A MARSHALL GARDEN GUIDE

CHOOSING PERENNIALS

A MARSHALL GARDEN GUIDE

CHOOSING PERENNIALS

Planting and maintaining a beautiful easy-care garden

Susan McClure

MARSHALL PUBLISHING • LONDON

A QUARTO BOOK

First published in the UK in 1998 by
Marshall Publishing Ltd
170 Piccadilly
London W1V 9DD

ISBN 1 84028 110 3

This book was designed and produced by
Quarto Publishing plc
The Old Brewery
6 Blundell Street
London N7 9BH

International Consultant: Barbara Haynes
Managing Editor: Sally MacEachern
Senior Editor: Louisa McDonnell
Editor: Sally Roth
Editorial Director: Mark Dartford
Indexer: Dorothy Frame
Senior Art Editor: Antonio Toma
Designer: Jessica Caws
Picture Researcher: Giulia Hetherington
Interior Illustrators: Dick Barnard, Robin Griggs,
Wayne Ford, Michelle Draycott
Art Director: Moira Clinch

Typeset in Great Britain by Central Southern Typesetters
Manufactured in Singapore by Universal Graphics Pte Ltd
Printed in Singapore by Star Standard Industries (Pte) Ltd

Contents

How to Use This Book

Once you begin planting perennials, you'll discover that they're true garden friends. Every spring, you can look forward to the pleasure of getting reacquainted as your perennials send up fresh green foliage and a dazzling display of flowers.

One of the best ways to enjoy perennials is in an easy-care perennial garden – one that looks wonderful, but takes minimal care. The secret to a successful and easy-care perennial garden is advance planning: choosing the right plants, preparing your site properly, and putting the plants together in a pleasing design. If you pay attention to these three basics, you can have a beautiful, easy-care garden. All the information you need to do just that is in this book.

Choosing Perennials has three parts, each of which can help you attain your goal of a beautiful easy-care perennial garden.

● If you'd like to browse through a potpourri of wonderful designs, any of which may be exactly what your garden needs, see "Easy-Care Garden Designs" beginning on page 8. If you have a sunny site in mind, turn to the Intriguing Island Bed on page 16, the Colour Theme Gardens on page 22, or the Colonial Cottage Garden on page 40. For a design that includes roses, check out the Romantic Perennial, Herb, and Rose Garden on page 34 and the Dynamic Driveway Border on page 46.

Perhaps you need a design for a shaded site. You'll find ideas in A Perennial Foundation Planting on page 10 and A Fabulous Four-Season Garden on page 52. For a shady garden under trees, consider A Serene Shade Garden on page 28.

When you find a design you like, be sure to turn to the following page. There you'll find garden options – suggestions for changing garden sizes or colour schemes, or substituting sun plants for shade.

● Before you embark on planting your garden, you need to know what it takes to grow perennials. Consult "Easy-Care Basics" starting on page 58. It covers all the techniques for perennial growing, from soil preparation and choosing plants to propagation and pest control.

● You'll need the details on caring for specific perennials after you've planted your garden, whether you use a design from this book or your own design. The "Easy-Care Perennial Encyclopedia" beginning on page 78 covers 60 terrific perennials. You'll find descriptions of the best easy-care species and cultivars, suggestions on how to use and combine the plants in gardens, and special tips on the kind of site and care each plant needs to look its best.

There's nothing more satisfying than a successful perennial garden. Each year, it returns looking better than the year before. With *Choosing Perennials*, you're guaranteed success. Your only problem may be deciding *which* wonderful garden you want to try first!

▶ **Yellow coreopsis** and red crocosmias are a colorful duo for an easy-care perennial garden.

Easy-Care Garden Designs

There's nothing as beautiful as a carefully designed perennial garden. You see them in glossy photos in magazines and books and wonder how you could ever have a garden as gorgeous as that. Actually, there's a trick that makes it possible for anyone to have a beautiful garden filled with colourful perennials. The trick is to start with a good design, then use tough, easy-care perennials that don't need a lot of pampering to look their best. To show you just how great looking easy-care perennials can be, I got together with three other perennial garden designers to create eight exciting and fun perennial gardens. To start with, designers Alexander Apanius, Robin Siktberg, Bobbie Schwartz, and I chose many of our favourite easy-care perennials – plants with beautiful blooms, attractive foliage and form, and the ability to thrive simply if given the right amount of sun or shade and reasonably decent soil.

We settled on a reliable cast of 60 easy-care perennials, plus a few additional plants for special situations. Then we came up with layouts for traditional and innovative perennial gardens for all kinds of gardens and both big and little spaces. You're sure to find a garden – or several! – that's perfect for you.

Each design illustrates how to pair up compatible plants, develop a sequence of bloom, and combine plants with different heights, textures, and flower colours to create a satisfying garden. I've also suggested ways to adapt each garden to add your own personality. I'll show you how to change the length, width, colour, and more to customize the design to your garden. Finally, each scheme includes a project – something you can make or do to make your garden even more beautiful and enjoyable.

With the great designs you'll find here, any time is a good time to start thinking about and planning a perennial garden!

A Perennial Foundation Planting

*If the foundation of your house is a victim of sad-shrub syndrome,
treat it to a perennial makeover. Drifts of beautiful easy-care perennials can make the most ordinary front
garden something special. The perennials soften the stark form of woody plants and bring a riot of spring
and summer colour to brighten the front of your house.*

This Perennial Foundation Planting fits comfortably on the north side of a bungalow or two-storey house. Landscaping a north-facing house front can be a challenge because of the mix of sun and shade conditions. This planting rises to the challenge with a mix of sun- and shade-loving perennials. Perennials for shade cluster near the house, while perennials for sun grow in island beds. A climber-clad trellis stretches up the wall beside a picture window. This design makes a beautiful finished picture, but if it seems too elaborate, try breaking out just a few of the beds to plant. Or, rework the plan to fit the shape and exposure of your house, as described on pages 12 and 13.

▼ **A mix of evergreen shrubs** makes a wonderful backdrop for the easy-care perennials in this foundation planting. Sweeps of moss phlox and epimediums are just one of many wonderful flowering combinations that this foundation garden offers.

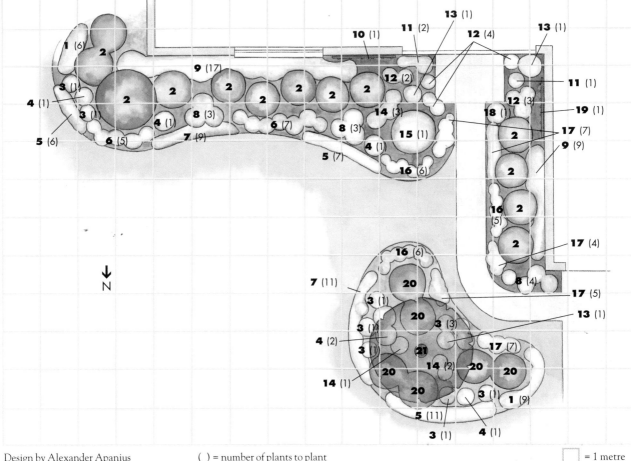

Design by Alexander Apanius   ( ) = number of plants to plant   ☐ = 1 metre

The Planting Plan. Many of the plants in the Perennial Foundation Planting will spread as they grow, reducing or eliminating weeding. Because their topgrowth dies back during winter, there is the fresh new growth to look forward to in the spring. None of the perennials in this planting need staking, and all are virtually pest-free. The island bed at the curve of the entry walk is optional. The Sargent's weeping hemlock is a small tree with overlapping arching branches. It does best in moist soil and will eventually reach 2 metres tall. See page 15 for more information on clematis.

1 'Sulphureum' epimedium (*Epimedium* × *versicolor* 'Sulphureum')

2 Existing shrubs

3 'Zagreb' coreopsis (*Coreopsis verticillata* 'Zagreb')

4 'Happy Returns' daylily (*Hemerocallis* 'Happy Returns')

5 Mixed violet-, pink-, and white-flowered moss phlox (*Phlox subulata*)

6 'Wargrave Pink' cranesbill (*Geranium* × *oxonianum* 'Wargrave Pink')

7 'Variegatum' sedum (*Sedum spurium* 'Variegatum') with

Siberian squill (*Scilla siberica*)

8 'Sprite' astilbe (*Astilbe* 'Sprite')

9 Lily-of-the-valley (*Convallaria majalis*)

10 Pink early-flowering clematis (*Clematis montana* var. *rubens*)

11 Brunnera (*Brunnera macrophylla*)

12 'Roy Davidson' lungwort (*Pulmonaria* 'Roy Davidson')

13 'So Sweet' hosta (*Hosta* 'So Sweet')

14 'Luxuriant' bleeding heart (*Dicentra* 'Luxuriant')

15 Sargent's weeping hemlock (*Tsuga canadensis* 'Pendula')

16 Bressingham Hybrids coral bells (*Heuchera* Bressingham Hybrids)

17 'Burgundy Glow' ajuga (*Ajuga reptans* 'Burgundy Glow') with 'Tête-à-Tête' daffodil (*Narcissus* 'Tête-à-Tête')

18 Christmas rose (*Helleborus niger*)

19 'Henryi' clematis (*Clematis* 'Henryi')

20 Creeping junipers

21 Japanese maple

STARTING FROM SCRATCH

Sometimes slow-growing shrubs like yews get so overgrown they just aren't right for the site anymore. They cover window views or block walkways. Your best choice may be to cut them down and start again Or, if you've bought a new house, it may not have a foundation planting at all.

If you decide to lay your foundation bare before planting the Perennial Foundation Planting (or if you live in a newly built home that isn't landscaped), here are some well-behaved woody plants that will work well in the design:

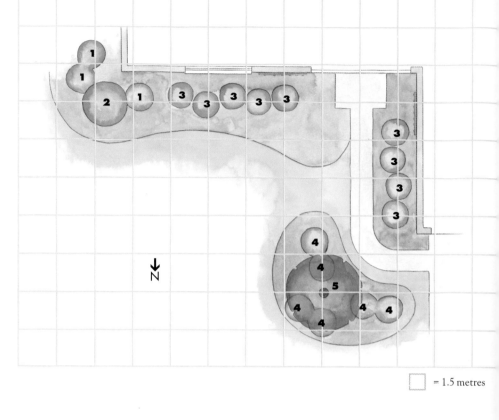

= 1.5 metres

1 Skimmia (*Skimmia japonica*)

2 'Shasta' viburnum (*Viburnum plicatum* 'Shasta')

3 'Nova Zembla' rhododendron (*Rhododendron* 'Nova Zembla')

4 'Blue Pacific' shore juniper (*Juniperus conferta* 'Blue Pacific')

5 'Bloodgood' Japanese maple (*Acer palmatum* 'Bloodgood')

Skimmias: Shiny, deep green leaves with clusters of pink or greenish flowers, and red berries if you plant male and female cultivars. They grow up to 1 metre tall and wide.

'Shasta' viburnum: This viburnum has very large white flowers and lovely reddish purple foliage in autumn. It reaches 2 metres tall and 3 metres wide when mature.

'Nova Zembla' rhododendron: This rhododendron sports dark red flowers. It grows to 1.5 metres tall and wide and like all rhododendrons requires an acid soil.

'Blue Pacific' shore juniper: A low-growing juniper with silver-blue foliage that spreads slowly to form a dense mat.

'Bloodgood' Japanese maple: The graceful form and red-purple, finely cut leaves make this Japanese maple a must. It will grow slowly to reach 4 to 4.5 metres tall.

All of these shrubs are hardy. Whenever you're shopping for trees or shrubs, always check with your supplier about hardiness, soil requirements and light requirements *before* you buy to save yourself from an expensive mistake.

MORE SHRUB CHOICES Of course, the shrubs listed above aren't the only ones you can use in the Perennial Foundation Planting. You may want to check the selection at local garden centres and nurseries and choose your own just-right shrubs. Or, pick from the following to substitute for the shrubs named above.

Skimmia alternatives: Mountain laurel (*Kalmia latifolia*) gives a beautiful floral display in spring and has excellent evergreen foliage. Try a mix of pink-flowered cultivars in place of skimmias, but keep in mind that mountain laurel requires cool, acid, moist, well-drained soil to grow well. Another evergreen alternative is 'Green Gem' a hybrid box (*Buxus* 'Green Gem'), which produces low mounds of dense dark green foliage.

Viburnum alternatives: Fragrant viburnum (*Viburnum carlesii*), which has delightfully scented white flowers, is an excellent choice for backyard gardens. You could also try 'Abel Carrière' weigela (*Weigela* 'Abel Carrière'), a prolific bloomer that produces bright pink flowers in spring. Purple-leaved cherry (*Prunus × cistena*) has pink flowers and attractive bronze leaves.

Rhododendron alternatives: If bright red flowers aren't to your taste, try white-flowered 'Album' Catawba rhododendron (*Rhododendron* 'Catawbiense Album') or 'Roseum Elegans' rhododendron (*R*. 'Roseum Elegans'), a fast-growing, rounded shrub with lilac-rose blooms.

Shore juniper alternatives: Some cultivars of yew are excellent foundation plants. One of the best is the elegant, low-growing 'Repandens' yew (*Taxus baccata* 'Repandens').

Japanese maple alternatives: Paperbark maple (*Acer griseum*) grows up to 6 metres tall and 4.5 metres wide and has cinnamon-brown peeling bark for year-round interest. Amur maple (*A. tataricum* subsp. *ginnala*) grows 3 to 5 metres tall and wide, has colourful autumn foliage, and is extremely hardy. Sourwood (*Oxydendrum arboreum*) has brilliant autumn colour. It is a slow-growing tree (to 2 metres in 15 years), but eventually can grow to 7 metres tall. Train as a multistemmed shrub for mixed plantings. Fringe tree (*Chionanthus virginicus*) prefers acid soil and grows to 3 metres tall. It has loose clusters of white flowers that mature to blue grapelike fruit on female trees. Pagoda dogwood (*Cornus alternifolia*) has white flowers and blue-black fruit; it reaches 6 metres tall and 4 metres wide.

◀ **For a shady foundation planting,** rely on hostas to add interesting leaf colour and texture. Try combining them with evergreen shrubs. A favourite garden ornament can also give your foundation garden that special touch.

BUILDING A TRELLIS It's easy to make a trellis like the ones used in the Perennial Foundation Planting. Each trellis is 2 metres wide and 1.5 metres high with a grid pattern.

You will need:

- 11 1.5-metre-long cedar 1 × 2s (25 × 50mm)
- 9 2 metre-long cedar 1 × 2s (25 × 50mm)
- 115 no. 6 × 50mm stainless steel screws
- Stain or paint
- 2 1.5-metre-long 2 × 4s (50 × 100mm)
- 2 2-metre-long 2 × 4s (50 × 100mm)
- 8 100mm oval brads
- 2 2.5-metre-long 4 × 4 posts (100 × 100mm)
- 8 no. 8 × 80mm stainless steel screws
- Electric drill

1 Lay out the cedar strips on a driveway, patio, or garage floor. Arrange the 1.5-metre-long strips (the vertical 1 × 2s) first. Then lay the 2-metre strips on top of them to form a grid. The openings in the grid should be about 15cm square.

2 Predrill a 2mm hole in each junction of the strips. Then screw the strips together with stainless steel screws.

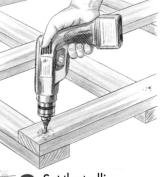

3 Set the trellis upright against a wall, and stain or paint the trellis to match the colour of your house.

4 On a level surface, lay out the 2 × 4s on edge to make a rectangular frame for the trellis. Nail the 2 × 4s together with the oval brads, two per corner.

5 Lay the trellis on the frame. Predrill holes in the left and right sides of the trellis through to the frame. Make holes in the vertical strips only. Screw the trellis to the frame.

6 Erect two 4 × 4 posts 1.5 metres apart where you plan to plant climbers. Sink about 75cm of the posts into the ground, leaving about 1.75 metres above ground.

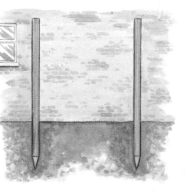

7 Stand the trellis upright against the posts, with the 2 × 4s touching the posts. Use scrap lumber to raise the trellis about 10cm off the ground. Drive two 80mm stainless steel screws at an angle through the upper face of the top 2 × 4 into each post. Then repeat at the bottom, driving the screws at an angle through the lower face of the bottom 2 × 4.

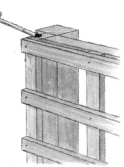

◀ **Bold clematis** flowers and trumpet-shaped goldflame honeysuckle blossoms make a great late summer combination for a sunny trellis.

GROWING CLIMBERS ON TRELLISES Perennial climbers have long twining or clinging stems that require a little special care. Climbers that twine or hang by tendrils, such as clematis and porcelain vine, require support and tend to stay put on a trellis. Others, such as Boston ivy (*Parthenocissus tricuspidata*), Virginia creeper (*P. quinquefolia*), and euonymus, can cling to and climb many surfaces, including your house and your shrubs. They may spread to cover a wider area than you planned including into your gutters unless you prune them vigorously. Feel free to thin out old or crowded growth or remove aggressively spreading sections. Time pruning of flowering climbers so you don't cut off all the flower buds. For summer-flowerers like honeysuckle, prune in late winter to early spring. Some types of clematis flower in spring, others in summer. Their pruning requirements are a little more specialized, so ask your supplier for specific pruning directions for the type of clematis you're buying.

CLIMBERS FOR A SUNNY TRELLIS. Here are some great climbers for a foundation garden in sun or light shade, such as the north side of a single-storey bungalow or sunny east, west, or south exposures of a house.

Akebia (*Akebia quinata*): This climber's brownish purple flowers are not showy, but they are fragrant. They are followed by purple berries on vines up to 9 metres.

Goldflame honeysuckle (*Lonicera*; × *heckrottii* 'Goldflame'): Reddish purple trumpet-shaped flowers with orange-yellow interiors open from summer into autumn on these twiners, which grow from 3 to 8 metres.

Pink montana clematis (*Clematis montana* var. *rubens*): Abundant light pink flowers with vanilla fragrance appear on this clematis in early summer. Stems can reach 6 metres.

Ampelopsis (*Ampelopsis brevipedunculata*): This climber sports clusters of pea-sized berries that change from lilac to porcelain blue in autumn.

'Jackmanii Superba' clematis (*Clematis* 'Jackmanii Superba'): This clematis has large, handsome violet-blue flowers that appear in late summer on stems up to 3 metres.

Sweet autumn clematis (*Clematis terniflora*): This vigorous grower reaches up to 3 metres. It has fragrant white flowers in late summer and early autumn that mature into attractive seedheads.

CLIMBERS FOR A SHADED TRELLIS. These climbers are perfect for foundation gardens on the shady side of two-storey homes.

'Lowii' Boston ivy (*Parthenocissus tricuspidata* 'Lowii'): This cultivar has three-lobed ivylike leaves. It is similar to Virginia creeper but grows more slowly. It also has spectacular red autumn colour.

Virginia creeper (*Parthenocissus quinquefolia*): The five-lobed leaves, which turn brilliant red in autumn, are the best feature of this vine, which can grow to 10 metres or more.

Euonymus (*Euonymus fortunei*): This glossy-leaved evergreen comes in a showy variegated form and can grow to 6 metres or more.

AN INTRIGUING ISLAND BED

To brighten a strategic corner of your garden, plant a freestanding, kidney-shaped island bed of sun-loving perennials.

Creating an island bed is an easy, fun project, especially for beginning perennial gardeners. Unlike a traditional perennial border set against a hedge or wall, an island bed is surrounded by open space. The gently curving outline of an island bed fits gracefully into the landscape. It's especially satisfying to stroll leisurely around a well-designed perennial island bed, noticing and enjoying the changing view of flowers and foliage from each point.

The Intriguing Island Bed is designed to be placed near a driveway, path, or patio, close enough so you can enjoy the cool lavender and blue flowers. Because you would view this bed mostly from one side, it has the tallest flowers planted at the "back" – the side farthest from the path, patio, or other main vantage point.

This garden has plenty of colour and interest all season long, beginning with spring-blooming bulbs including daffodils and Siberian squill. The tall blue flower spikes of Russian sage, the tallest plant in the garden, appear in summer and last for more than one month. Autumn brings more lovely blossoms of Frikart's aster, and the dried seedheads of 'Autumn Joy' sedum look beautiful through the winter.

▲ **As spring turns** to summer in this island bed, daffodils and other bulbs fade back, hidden by the fresh foliage of other perennials. The blue flowers of Siberian iris and purple-leaved ajuga hint at the floral display to come.

The Planting Plan. It's a good idea to use an edging of plastic, metal, or brick to keep lawngrasses from creeping into the bed. Remove the fading flowers on verbena, cranesbill 'A.T. Johnson', 'Happy Returns' daylily, and Frikart's aster to encourage a long bloom period. Frikart's aster may droop when in bloom and can look lovely cascading over the nearby silvery mound of artemisia. But if you prefer it upright, pinch the shoots back in spring to make the plant grow lower and bushier. If the artemisia tends to flop open from the centre, divide it and avoid fertilizing it.

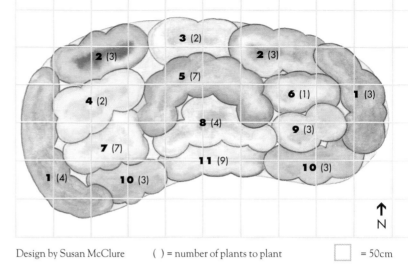

Design by Susan McClure   ( ) = number of plants to plant   ☐ = 50cm

1 Verbena (*Verbena corymbosa*)

2 'Caesar's Brother' Siberian iris (*Iris sibirica* 'Caesar's Brother')

3 'Pink Damask' daylily (*Hemerocallis* 'Pink Damask') or other tall pink-flowered daylily with daffodils (*Narcissus*)

4 Russian sage (*Perovskia atriplicifolia*)

5 'Autumn Joy' sedum (*Sedum* 'Herbstfreude')

6 Early-flowering daylily (*Hemerocallis lilioasphodelus*) or other tall pale daylily with daffodils

7 'Happy Returns' daylily (*Hemerocallis* 'Happy Returns') with daffodils

8 'A.T. Johnson' cranesbill (*Geranium × oxonianum* 'A.T. Johnson') with daffodils

9 Frikart's aster (*Aster × frikartii*)

10 'Nana' artemisia (*Artemisia schmidtiana* 'Nana')

11 Purple-leaved ajuga (*Ajuga reptans* 'Atropurpurea') with white Siberian squill (*Scilla siberica*)

▲ **In midsummer,** flowers of pink cranesbill 'A.T. Johnson' and rose verbena may linger on, while a medley of daylilies joins the tall blue spikes of Russian sage. Lavender-blue Frikart's aster adds to the summer show. Pink flowers may start to appear on 'Autumn Joy' sedum.

REARRANGING THE VIEWS If you want to plant the Intriguing Island Bed where you can view it from all sides, reposition the plants so the high point will be in the centre. Russian sage is the tallest perennial in this design, so plant it in the centre. Place the medium-height Frikart's aster and 'Autumn Joy' sedum along the boundary of the bed instead of Siberian iris, which will occupy the spot where the Russian sage would have been. The garden remains edged with low silver-foliaged artemisia and purple-leaved ajuga across the front and medium-height rose verbena along the sides. The blue Russian sage and Siberian iris and the tall pink daylilies form a flowering high point in the middle with modest-sized, yellow 'Happy Returns' daylily, pink cranesbill 'A.T. Johnson', and lavender Frikart's aster at their feet.

WHERE SHOULD YOUR ISLAND GO? There's almost no limit to the possible sites for a perennial island. You can use island beds to define the boundaries of your garden and to create privacy. They are wonderful for separating parts of your garden that you use for different purposes – such as an outdoor sitting area from your vegetable garden or the children's swing set. They provide a splash of colour you can enjoy from your windows, and they make a handsome main attraction when you entertain on the patio. Use island beds near the corner of a patio or along a path or boundary line. Stretch island beds under some shade trees or around a cluster of shrubs to make them into a garden feature rather than isolated plants, and to cut down on mowing chores as well.

Sun-drenched areas are ideal for growing the sturdy sun-loving perennials in the Intriguing Island Bed. Island beds around trees or clusters of shrubs are great for perennials that prefer shade. If you plan to create several island beds in your garden, be sure to use a similar colour scheme or some of the same plants, so that the beds have a common thread.

▶ **It's easy** to reposition the plants in the Intriguing Island Bed so that it can be viewed from all sides. Just follow this revised planting plan to make a few changes that place the taller plants in the centre of the bed.

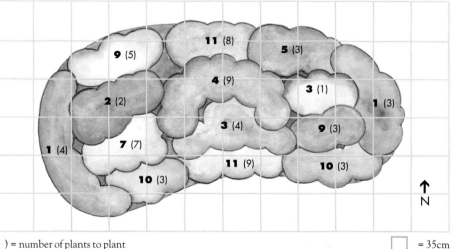

( ) = number of plants to plant   ☐ = 35cm

1 Verbena (*Verbena corymbosa*)

2 'Caesar's Brother' Siberian iris (*Iris sibirica* 'Caesar's Brother')

3 'Pink Damask' daylily (*Hemerocallis* 'Pink Damask') or other tall pink-flowered daylily with daffodils (*Narcissus*)

4 Russian sage (*Perovskia atriplicifolia*)

5 'Autumn Joy' sedum (*Sedum* 'Herbstfreude')

6 Early-flowering daylily (*Hemerocallis lilioasphodelus*) or other tall pale daylily with daffodils

7 'Happy Returns' daylily (*Hemerocallis* 'Happy Returns') with daffodils

8 'A.T. Johnson' cranesbill (*Geranium* × *oxonianum* 'A.T. Johnson') with daffodils

9 Frikart's aster (*Aster* × *frikartii*)

10 'Nana' artemisia (*Artemisia schmidtiana* 'Nana')

11 Purple-leaved ajuga (*Ajuga reptans* 'Atropurpurea') with white Siberian squill (*Scilla siberica*)

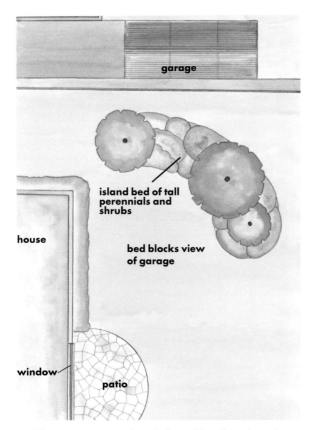

▲ **Plant a sweeping island bed** at the edge of your garden to block an undesirable view.

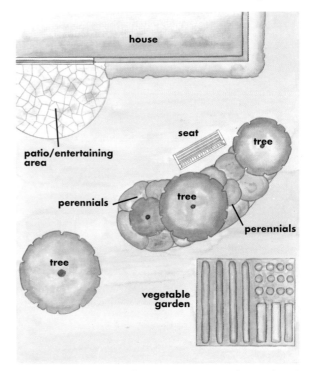

▲ **Separate "outdoor rooms"** with an island bed. For example, you can use a perennial island as the wall between a patio sitting area and a work area that includes your vegetable garden.

TIPS FOR DESIGNING YOUR OWN ISLAND BED

Want to try designing an island bed from scratch? It's easy to do. Here are a few simple guidelines to follow:

● For an appealing sense of proportion, make your island bed two to four times longer than it is wide. For example, a 3-metre-wide bed looks well proportioned if it's 6 to 12 metres long.

● Limit the height of the tallest perennials in the bed to about half the width of the bed. For example, if the bed is 1.5 metres wide, plan on using perennials that top out at about 75cm tall.

● The organization of the perennials in the bed will vary depending on your main vantage point. If you'll view the island bed equally from all sides, put the tallest perennials in the centre of the bed and layer shorter perennials around them. If you see the garden primarily from one direction, put the taller perennials

closer to the back and build layers of lower plants in the foreground.

● In an island bed set beneath a tree, let the tallest perennials billow around the base of the tree.

● Cut down on planting time and expense in a large island bed by using perennial groundcovers that spread quickly and are easy to multiply by division. Let low groundcovers, such as moss phlox (*Phlox subulata*), cruise across the front and rear of an island bed. Fill the interior of the bed with taller spreading perennials such as daylilies (*Hemerocallis*).

● Avoid aggressively spreading perennials like mints (*Mentha*) in island beds. They can quickly overwhelm the other plants.

PROPAGATING PERENNIAL GROUNDCOVERS

Perennial groundcovers are a great choice for an easy-to-plant, low-care island bed. They're especially useful in a shady bed, where you can plant shade-tolerant ground-covers like hostas, ferns, and lily-of-the-valley to add colour and brightness. Whether you're planting in sun or shade, if you propagate your own, you can create beautiful beds for very little money. It's a snap to multiply perennial groundcovers by dividing them, especially groundcovers such as bugle (*Ajuga*), *Artemisia ludoviciana* 'Silver Queen', creeping phlox and moss phlox, and others that expand by sending out shoots or roots that creep on or near the soil surface. The best time to divide is during spring and autumn, when the plants are emerging from dormancy or about to die back to the ground for winter. For best results, try to divide several months before the perennial usually flowers or before the weather gets severely hot, cold, or dry. (For more on timing, see page 75.)

STARTING A NEW GROUNDCOVER BED STEP-BY-STEP

1 With a sharp trowel or spade, slice through the plant and soil between the main part of the plant and plantlet. Lift the plantlet, keeping as much soil around the roots as you can.

2 Set the plantlets into a seed tray or wheelbarrow. It's best to replant them right away. If you can't, wet the roots with a fine spray from the can, cover the shoots, and

move them into a cool, shady spot where they can be kept for a few hours or overnight.

3 If you have a large bed to fill with these new plants, gently pull apart the plantlets into single plants, making sure each piece is well supplied with

roots and greenery. For smaller spaces, or if you have an abundance of plants, keep the divisions large so they fill out fast.

4 Set the plants in natural-looking groups that wind through the bed, planting them at the same height as they were growing previously. Make

sure low-growing perennials are in the foreground and taller perennials are toward the centre of the bed. Plant slow-spreading perennials like lady's-mantle 30cm apart. Space fast spreaders like lily-of-the-valley up to 30cm apart.

5 Spread a 5-cm layer of organic mulch, like compost, leaf mould, or composted bark, around the new plants, and water them well.

Check them frequently after planting, and keep them moist until they begin to grow vigorously again. Small divisions or plantlets with few roots may need extra coddling.

GROUND-COVERING PERENNIALS

If you've got space to cover, you'll want to try some of these great perennial groundcovers. All of them are easy to divide. You'll find more information about these perennials in Part 3 of this book.

PLANT NAMES	RATE OF SPREAD	RANGE OF HEIGHT
For Sun		
Achillea (Yarrows)	Moderate	30–150cm
Ajuga (Bugles)	Moderate to fast	5–30cm
Alchemilla mollis (Lady's-mantle)	Slow	20–30cm
Artemisia ludoviciana 'Silver Queen'	Fast	75–120cm
Hemerocallis (Daylilies)	Moderate	35–150cm
Sedum album	Moderate	10–15cm
Sedum kamtschaticum	Moderate	3–15cm
Verbena tenuisecta	Moderate	10–20cm
For Light Shade		
Ajuga (Bugles)	Moderate to fast	5–30cm
Alchemilla mollis (Lady's-mantle)	Slow	20–30cm
Asarum (Wild gingers)	Moderate	15–30cm
Convallaria majalis (Lily-of-the-valley)	Fast	15–20cm
Epimedium	Moderate	15–35cm
Geranium macrorrhizum (Cranesbill)	Fast	35–40cm
Hemerocallis (Daylilies)	Moderate	35–150cm
Mentha (Mints)	Fast	2–90cm
Phlox stolonifera (Creeping phlox)	Moderate	15–25cm
Polygonatum (Solomon's seals)	Moderate	30–200cm
Pulmonaria (Lungworts)	Moderate	25–40cm
Tiarella cordifolia (Foamflower)	Moderate	15–25cm
Viola (Violets)	Moderate	3–30cm

Sedum kamtschaticum

Hemerocallis fulva 'Green Kwanso'

Solomon's seal

Pulmonaria

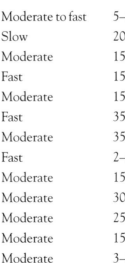

'Rose Queen' epimedium

Colour Theme Gardens

Planting a perennial colour theme garden is a great way to learn how to create beautiful plant combinations and how to plan a garden that has colour and interest all season long.

What would a perennial garden be without colour? Colours set the mood of a garden and bring it to life. With colour theme perennial gardens, your options are nearly limitless. You can create a garden around a single colour, choose two strongly contrasting colours, or make a rainbow garden of mixed colours. And if you're interested in developing your own colour theme perennial bed, turn to page 26 for directions on creating an original garden design.

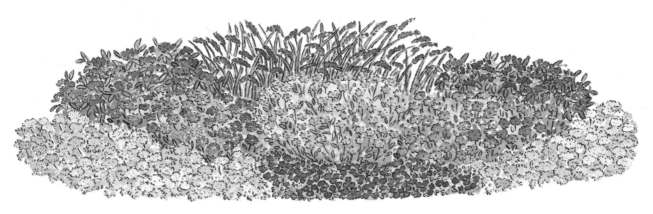

Planting Plan for a Hot Colour Garden. This garden mixes bold, bright flowers in an island bed designed to be viewed from all sides.

cultivar)

1 'Lucifer' crocosmia (*Crocosmia* 'Lucifer') with daffodils (*Narcissus*)

2 Butterfly weed (*Asclepias tuberosa*) with daffodils (*Narcissus*)

3 Woolly yarrow (*Achillea tomentosa*)

4 Pink tickseed (*Coreopsis rosea*)

5 'Early Sunrise' coreopsis (*Coreopsis grandiflora* 'Early Sunrise') with daffodils (*Narcissus*)

6 'Scarlet Flame' moss phlox (*Phlox subulata* 'Scarlet Flame') or scarlet pansies (*Viola* × *wittrockiana* cultivar)

▲ **Summer is hot** in this garden of rich red, brassy pink, and brilliant yellow flowers.

Design by Susan McClure   ( ) = number of plants to plant   ☐ = 45cm

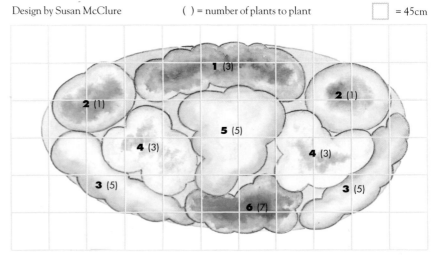

Planting Plan for a Warm Garden.
If you like sunny, vivid colours,
you'll enjoy this garden of pure
yellow and red flowers. Rose lovers
will opt to plant 'Scarlet Meidiland'
roses, while peony lovers will
choose the spring colour and
fragrance of peony blossoms. For
more information on 'Scarlet
Meidiland' roses, see page 35. If
peony bloom declines over time,
it's a sign that the plants are
overcrowded. Lift the clumps in
late summer, divide them, and
replant. 'Moonbeam' coreopsis will
bloom much of the summer and
into autumn if deadheaded.
'September Ruby' aster will need
staking for support.

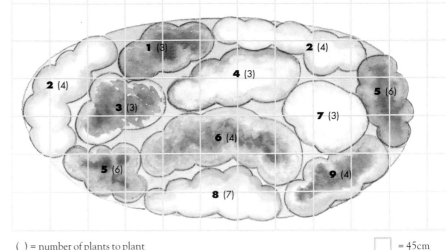

( ) = number of plants to plant   = 45cm

1 'September Ruby' New England
aster (*Aster novae-angliae*
'Septemberrubin')

2 'Moonbeam' coreopsis
(*Coreopsis verticillata* 'Moonbeam')

3 'Stafford' daylily (*Hemerocallis*
'Stafford') or 'Lucifer' crocosmia
(*Crocosmia* 'Lucifer')

4 'Hoffnung' yarrow
(*Achillea* 'Hoffnung')

5 'Palace Purple' heuchera
(*Heuchera micrantha* var. *diversifolia*
'Palace Purple')

6 Red-flowered hybrid peony
(*Paeonia* hybrid) or 'Scarlet
Meidiland' rose (*Rosa* 'Scarlet
Meidiland') with daffodils
(*Narcissus*)

7 'Paprika' yarrow
(*Achillea millefolium* 'Paprika')

8 'Red Spangles' coral bells
(*Heuchera* 'Red Spangles') with red
and yellow tulips (*Tulipa*)

9 'Jenny' Michaelmas daisy
(*Aster novi- belgii* 'Jenny')

▼ **Summer finds this garden** in
top form with red and soft yellow
yarrows, airy yellow coreopsis
blossoms, red roses and daylilies,
and delicate coral bells in the
foreground.

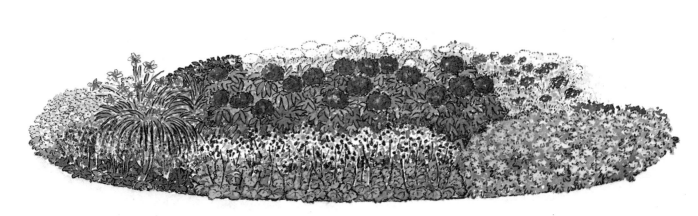

Planting Plan for a Garden with Contrasting Colours. If you're looking for truly eye-catching combinations, try this design featuring blue-, yellow-, and white-flowering perennials and bulbs. The jonquils and daffodils provide early colour, and the developing perennials will hide the bulb foliage as it dies back. The compact 'Purple Dome' asters should not need staking. If your garden has very rich soil, the salvia may tend to flop if not supported. If you choose to plant blue false indigo instead of Siberian iris, plant only four plants.

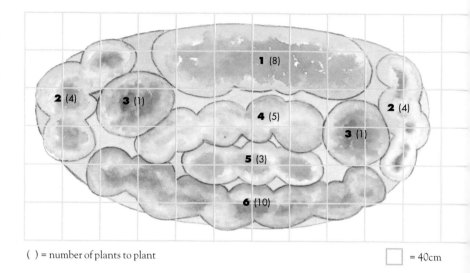

( ) = number of plants to plant

□ = 40cm

1 Purple or blue variety of Siberian iris (*Iris sibirica*) or blue false indigo (*Baptisia australis*) with trumpet daffodils (*Narcissus*)

2 'East Friesland' salvia (*Salvia nemorosa* 'Ostbriesland')

3 'Hidcote' lavender (*Lavandula angustifolia* 'Hidcote')

4 'Moonbeam' coreopsis (*Coreopsis verticillata* 'Moonbeam')

5 'Purple Dome' New England aster (*Aster novae-angliae* 'Purple Dome')

6 Purple-leaved ajuga (*Ajuga reptans* 'Atropurpurea') with jonquils (*Narcissus jonquilla*)

▼ **In late summer,** purple is the dominant colour in this contrasting garden, set off by the clear yellow blossoms of 'Moonbeam' coreopsis.

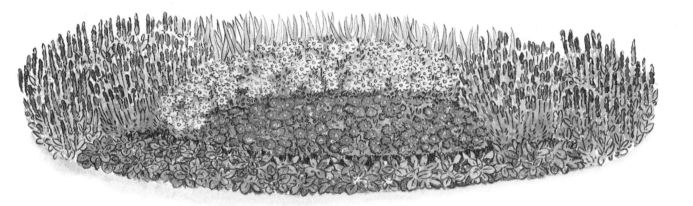

Early summer features airy sprays of crambe at the centre of the pastel garden. Thrift adds cheerful pink in front, flanked by blue and white cranesbills.

Planting Plan for a Pastel Garden. This garden features pink, blue, and white flowers, which always make great companions. Choose a mix of crocus cultivars that reflect this colour theme. 'Album' bloody cranesbill is a surprising white-flowered cultivar of this normally pink- or red-flowering perennial. Keep in mind that balloon flowers are slow to emerge in spring. Clip off fading blooms from balloon flowers and Stokes' asters to extend their bloom season into autumn.

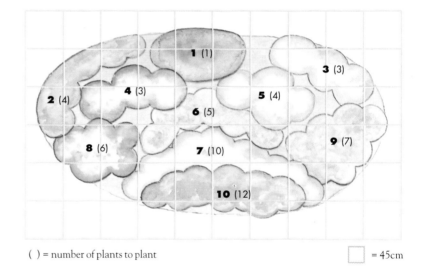

( ) = number of plants to plant   = 45cm

1 Crambe (*Crambe cordifolia*)

2 Blue-flowered balloon flower (*Platycodon grandiflorus*) with grape hyacinths (*Muscari*)

3 White-flowered balloon flower (*Platycodon grandiflorus* f. *albus*) with grape hyacinths (*Muscari*)

4 'Apple Blossom' yarrow (*Achillea millefolium* 'Apple Blossom')

5 'Margarete' Japanese anemone (*Anemone* × *hybrida* 'Margarete')

6 Blue-flowered Stokes' aster (*Stokesia laevis*)

7 White-flowered Stokes' aster (*Stokesia laevis* 'Alba')

8 'Album' bloody cranesbill (*Geranium sanguineum* 'Album')

9 'Johnson's Blue' cranesbill (*Geranium* × *oxonianum* 'Johnson's Blue')

10 Thrift (*Armeria maritima*) with crocuses (*Crocus*)

DEVELOPING YOUR OWN COLOUR THEME To get ideas for colour theme gardens, look at photographs of perennial gardens in books and magazines. Visit botanical gardens or the display gardens at a local nursery. You might even get ideas for colour combinations from a pretty wallpaper or fabric pattern – just let your imagination go!

Draw your own colour wheel like this one to help plan a colour theme garden. To find pairs of exciting contrasting colours, lay a ruler directly across the wheel. The two colours that the ruler touches, like yellow and violet, are contrasting. Adjacent colours, like blue and blue-green, are harmonious and calming.

If you like bold, bright gardens, choose flowers with contrasting colours such as violet and yellow, blue and orange, or red and green. For a more restful garden, mix colours that are close, such as yellow and orange or blue and violet.

Try setting cool colours in front of a warm-coloured background, such as blue flowers in front of red flowers. The contrast will make the cool colours more noticeable. Warm colours stand out even right at the back of the garden. To soften the warm colours, use pastels such as lemon yellow, apricot orange, or pink, and blend them with cooler colours.

When you create a colour theme garden, you can maintain the same colours throughout the growing season or let them change. For instance, a warm colour garden could feature sunny yellows and whites in spring, change to many colours in early summer, move to golds and violets in late summer, and then to fall crimsons and bronze.

MAKE A COLOUR VALUE FINDER A colour value finder is a homemade collection of colour samples. You can use it to keep track of the true colours of the perennials that you come across in gardens or at nurseries. This will help you when you select perennials for a colour theme garden.

To make a colour value finder, collect paint shade cards (you can get these at any DIY store) that show clear primary colours as well as more complex colours. You'll want to include yellow, yellow-green, green, blue-green, blue, blue-violet, violet, red-violet, red, orange-red, orange, and yellow-orange. The paint chips on the card will also show the pastel tints and darker shades of these colours. Each colour on a chip is identified by a name or number. (The names may be fanciful, like "Free Spirit" or "Bianca," rather than descriptive of the colour, but they'll still serve your purpose here.)

Staple or glue each colour patch on a separate piece of paper in a small notebook. Take the notebook along with you when you shop or visit a botanical garden. When you see a perennial that appeals to you, match its colour to one of the colours on a paint chip in your homemade colour value finder. Make a note of the plant name and colour.

When you're ready to plan a garden, pull out your colour value finder and your notes. By referring to the paint chips, you'll get a true picture of the colours you'll get in your garden and can group plants according to your tastes.

Keep an accurate record of the flower colours of perennials you've admired at gardens and nurseries with a colour value finder.

PICKING COLOUR THEME PLANTS You'll find lots of variety in the descriptions of flower colours in perennial catalogues and books. One source will call a certain flower scarlet while another calls it bright pink. It's best to confirm the colour of a perennial for yourself before you choose it for a garden. (One way to keep records of the true colours of perennials is with a colour value finder like the one described on the opposite page.)

When you're designing a colour theme garden, you'll want to start with two main colours. You may pick two of your favourite colours, or you may decide that your colour theme should pick up the colours of the interior of your home or of your exterior shutters or your paving.

The best combinations often come from pure colours – such as blue, red, orange, violet or yellow. But flowers with different undertones – such as salmon-pink and lavender-pink – usually clash. You can refer to the colour wheel on the opposite page to learn more about the relationships between colours.

Also consider leaf colour – dark green, purple, silver, chartreuse, gold, or even black – that can serve as a third accent colour or one of the two main colours. One easy way to maintain a unified colour theme over several seasons is to include a few long-flowering plants such as coreopsis or black-eyed Susans.

REFINING A COLOUR THEME GARDEN You can refine a colour theme garden even after it's planted and growing. You may decide that the colours aren't balanced. Perhaps there's too much violet in one half of the garden and hardly any in the other. Or you may decide you want yellow as an accent of colour that repeats throughout the design. After all, experimenting with colour is what a colour theme garden is all about.

If you do decide to change a garden, make notes about which plants you want to move or divide and where you'll move them to. Then wait until the plants finish blooming, and dig them up and replant them. Pamper them a bit until they reestablish themselves, and then wait to see how your new perennial colour picture turns out!

SKETCHING A GARDEN DESIGN Using catalogues, books, and your colour value finder with notes on perennial colours, select perennials with appropriate flower colours.

1 Use a pencil to sketch your garden site to scale on a piece of graph paper. The scale of 1cm to 50cm should work for most small or moderate-size gardens.

2 Draw circles and ovals in the garden to represent each type of perennial. Put the tallest perennial toward the rear of the garden. Then fill in a front edging of low-growing perennials. Add in more perennials from side to side, using a balanced blend of colours on either side. You can repeat clusters of the same plant or use different plants that have the same colours.

3 Put tracing paper over your garden plan, and use markers or coloured pencils to fill in the flower colours of the plants that will bloom in spring. Then take another piece of tracing paper and colour in the summer flowerers, and a third for the autumn bloomers. You may need to change some of your plant choices to ensure that the colours are nicely coordinated through the seasons.

A SERENE SHADE GARDEN

With easy-care perennials that love shade, you can turn a stark area under trees into a beautiful, colourful garden retreat.

Anemones, foamflowers, astilbes, goat's beard, bleeding hearts, and lily-of-the-valley all thrive in light shade. In the Serene Shade Garden, you'll find all of these lovely flowers, along with the handsome foliage of variegated Solomon's seal and Japanese painted fern.

Foliage texture and form also play an important role: divided leaves of anemones, toothed foamflower leaves, upright swordlike leaves of lily-of-the-valley, arching stems of Solomon's seal, heart-shaped epimedium foliage, and the bold, dark green leaves of black snakeroot. Together, they create a garden that lures you closer to investigate its subtle beauty. Shafts of light filtering through the tree branches overhead and the rustling of the leaves will add even more pleasure to your visit to the Serene Shade Garden.

▶ **Soft pastels** fill a woodland garden in spring. Spring-blooming shade perennials include epimedium, fragrant blue phlox, delicate white spikes of foamflower, bell-shaped Solomon's seal, and lily-of-the-valley blossoms.

The Planting Plan. This design features a pebbled path that loops around two shade trees, and a bench for sitting and enjoying the garden. The narrow planting beds are extra-easy to tend. Watch for slugs on the hostas, and keep the soil moist for top performance from astilbes, Solomon's seal, and foamflower.

1 'Margarete' Japanese anemone (*Anemone × hybrida* 'Margarete')

2 Astilbe (*Astilbe chinensis* var. *pumila*)

3 Blue phlox (*Phlox divaricata*)

4 Epimedium (*Epimedium*)

5 Wild bleeding heart (*Dicentra formosa*)

6 Black snakeroot (*Cimicifuga racemosa*)

7 'Rheinland' astilbe (*Astilbe* 'Rheinland')

8 Japanese painted fern (*Athyrium niponicum* 'Pictum')

9 Lily-of-the-valley (*Convallaria majalis*)

10 Solomon's seal (*Polygonatum biflorum*)

11 Hosta (*Hosta sieboldiana* var. *elegans*)

12 Goat's beard (*Aruncus dioicus*)

13 Foamflower (*Tiarella cordifolia*)

14 'Ginko Craig' hosta (*Hosta* 'Ginko Craig')

15 'Whirlwind' Japanese anemone (*Anemone × hybrida* 'Whirlwind')

16 Variegated Solomon's seal (*Polygonatum odoratum* 'Variegatum')

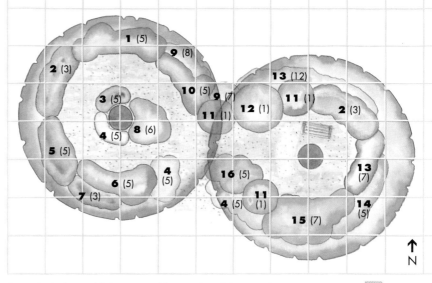

Design by Robin A. Siktberg ( ) = number of plants to plant ☐ = 65cm

▶ **Autumn brings red and yellow** to the trees that shelter the Serene Shade Garden. In the garden itself, the foliage of many perennials also turns a lovely yellow, and clouds of white anemone flowers emerge.

CREATING YOUR OWN SHADE Shade trees aren't an absolute requirement for creating a shade garden. You can plant a lovely shade garden under a pergola topped with lath or wooden beams. In fact, your plants may be happiest growing under a pergola, where they'll have light shade, but no tree roots competing for moisture and nutrients.

A pergola can be rustic or ornate, whatever matches your home and landscape. You can make a simple pergola by erecting two rows of 4 x 4 wooden posts and topping them with lath. Plant climbers such as clematis, trumpet creeper (*Campsis radicans*), hardy kiwi (*Actinidia arguta* 'Issai'), or mile-a-minute vine (*Fallopia aubertii*) by the posts; the plants will climb them and fill in overhead.

To adapt the Serene Shade Garden for planting under a pergola, choose a selection of the plants used, and group them in pleasing combinations. Choose the smaller perennials for best results – goat's beard (*Aruncus*), hostas and black snakeroot are so large that they would overwhelm the space underneath. Leave an open area in the centre for a piece of garden sculpture or a bench.

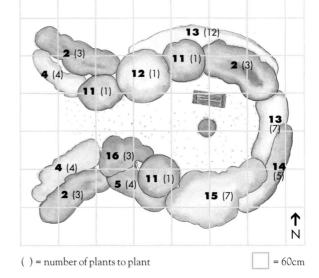

( ) = number of plants to plant   ☐ = 60cm

A GARDEN FOR A SINGLE TREE If you only have a single shade tree in your yard, adapt the plan for the Serene Shade Garden by planting half of the garden. Create an inviting entrance that guides visitors to the garden with curved beds of epimedium backed by astilbes. (Refer to page 29 for the list of plants.)

▶ **A wooden pergola** covered by climbers like trumpet creeper, clematis, and hardy kiwi creates a pretty setting for enjoying shade-loving perennials.

SCREENS FOR SHADE AND PRIVACY A fence or hedge that runs from east to west or from northwest to southeast will cast shade during a good portion of the day. Plant a shady perennial garden next to it, and you'll create a peaceful outdoor retreat where you can relax on weekends, visit with friends, or just sit and enjoy the flowers. A screen can divide different parts of your landscape, separating a quiet reading corner from your entertaining patio, and it can also make a nice backdrop for a garden.

Living screens include hedges, shrubs, and ornamental grasses. You can also screen areas with fences, walls, and trellises. Here are some points to consider when choosing a screen.

Evergreens. Plant a staggered double line of conifers such as cypress, thujas, or yew. In time, they will mature to form a solid wall of greenery. For immediate privacy, you'll need to start with large plants up to 1.5 metres tall. Your privacy will become more complete as the trees grow, even blocking views from your neighbour's second-storey windows.

Hedges. If you have time to let a hedge develop, it can be a lovely and relatively inexpensive alternative to fencing. A hedge of needle-leaved evergreens gives year-round screening and foliage interest. Some broad-leaved evergreens, such as rhododendrons or cherry laurels, also bear flowers. Deciduous shrubs, which hold their leaves only through the growing season, may be suitable if you only need privacy for fair-weather outdoor forays. Deciduous shrubs can be more interesting than evergreens, providing a progression of flowers, fruit, and autumn colour.

Shrub Clusters. A cluster of three or five shrubs can provide a perfect screen for a small open area. Shrub clusters are less expensive than hedges and can be more relaxed and natural looking – and they're also a lot less work.

Fences. Fences are a good choice when you want instant shade and privacy. A 1.5-metre-tall fence makes a nice screen. In a low-lying yard, you may need a taller fence. Fences do require some maintenance (especially wooden ones). Check local authority regulations about fences before you finalize your plans.

Walls. To create the impression of privacy without a tall fence, try building a low stone or brick wall, and create a garden beside it that includes some tall plants. For example, you could combine perennials with tall ornamental grasses like miscanthus, or plant shrubs and small ornamental trees like crab apples, dogwoods, sorbus, or viburnums.

Trellises. A tightly woven lattice lets in little of the outside world; an open lattice serves mostly as a symbolic garden wall. To make a more effective screen, plant climbers to fill the lattice, and then add perennials in front.

▲ **A mature evergreen hedge** creates a natural wall that screens noise and traffic and is a great backdrop for warm-coloured perennials.

▲ **Low-growing branches** on large shade trees can block so much light that it's hard to grow anything beneath them (*left*). Have a tree surgeon remove a few limbs to let in light and create a good garden site (*right*).

5 TRICKS TO BRING LIGHT TO YOUR SHADY SITE

Lots of lovely plants bloom in partial shade. But there just aren't many perennials that will bloom in deep shade. So if your garden seems dominated by dark, gloomy areas, try some of the following techniques to let in more light. Then you'll have a greater variety of shade-tolerant flowers to choose from when creating easy-care shade gardens.

Thin Out Undergrowth. If your shady area is tangled with young saplings and shrubs, very little light will reach the perennials below. Before preparing the garden bed in an overgrown area like this, cut back and remove some of the excess brush.

Limb Up Trees. Remove lower limbs on shade trees so that sunlight will reach the area underneath them in the morning and late afternoon. (Another benefit is that you won't run into the branches as you mow the lawn.) It's smart to call a professional tree surgeon for this type of job.

Thin Out Tree Limbs. To let light through thickly branched shade trees, consider having a professional tree surgeon thin branches. Direct your tree surgeon crews to cut out small and medium-sized branches to reduce foliage density. They can also remove any main limbs that arise directly under another branch or are crossing, rubbing, or diseased. A word of advice: NEVER ask an tree surgeon to top a tree or cut limbs back partway. This damages the tree, and the resulting bushy regrowth will block all light to the ground besides.

Start Smart. Some trees, such as *Genista aetnensis*, false acacia (*Robina pseudacacia*), honey locusts (*Gleditsia triacanthos*) and birches (*Betula*), have naturally open branching or fine leaves that allow some sun through without any extra pruning. If you are starting a shade garden from scratch, these are great trees to plant. Other deciduous trees, even those with heavy canopies, allow enough light through in spring before the tree leaves open to support the growth of spring-blooming bulbs. Most evergreen trees, however, cast heavy shade year-round.

Maximize Sunlight. Make the most of sunlight by planting where the sun shines the longest. Unless blocked by shadows, the sun touches only one side of a grove of trees all day. The other side of the grove will be in shadow most of the day and will have the least amount of sun.

6 WAYS TO MAKE DARK SPOTS SEEM BRIGHTER

Sometimes there's just no easy way to get more sun to a site – for example, when a solid building is what's blocking the sun. Here are some simple suggestions that will make a shady spot seem brighter.

Emphasize Light-Coloured Flowers. Select plants with bright white or light pastel flowers that reflect light and stand out in shadows. For maximum impact, choose perennials with large, open-faced flowers, such as anemones, or dense clusters of small flowers, such as astilbes. And don't turn your nose up at mixing in shade-tolerant annuals like white-flowered busy lizzies (*Impatiens*).

Dabble in Variegated Foliage. Many of the nicest hostas have foliage edged or marked with white or cream. Variegated Solomon's seal also gives dark areas the appearance of dappled sunlight. Bright flowers come and go through the seasons, but variegated foliage remains bright spring, summer, and autumn.

▲ **To transform a dreary corner,** plant a light-coloured planter like this urn with colourful, shade-tolerant impatiens.

◄ **Choose interesting foliage** to light up shady plantings such as variegated Solomon's seal and hostas.

Display Plants in Bright Pots. Highlight your shade garden with flowering or foliage plants in light-coloured pots. Choose from cement, reconstituted stone, or carved stone planters in white or light grey. Bring ceramic or stoneware pots inside when temperatures drop below freezing to prevent cracking.

Think White for Furniture and Structures. Bright white lawn furniture will glow in a shady garden sitting area. Light-coloured or painted wood on nearby trellises and pergolas will do the same.

Brighten the Scene with Light-Coloured Bark. Consider growing trees such as beeches or birches that have light-coloured bark. Beeches (*Fagus*) have tight, smooth silver bark. Easy-care monarch birch (*Betula maximowicziana*) has cinnamon-coloured bark that brightens to pale grey with maturity.

Pave the Path with White Stones. A path of light-coloured stones looks cool and inviting heading into a shady spot, while a dark gravel path just seems to disappear in shadows.

A ROMANTIC PERENNIAL, HERB, AND ROSE GARDEN

*You can create a beautiful, fragrant garden with plants to use in cooking
and crafts by combining easy-care perennials, roses, and herbs.*

This garden features a rainbow carpet of aromatic gold and silver oregano, thyme, lavender and sage. It also includes great perennials for cutting, drying and wreath making, such as yarrow, lady's-mantle, echinaceas, globe thistle, and sea holly. Most of these flowers will bloom from summer into autumn if you deadhead the old flowers regularly. The semiformal half-moon bed is perfect for planting beside a patio, where it will add a romantic and fragrant atmosphere when you sit outside to enjoy some time with special friends.

The Romantic Perennial, Herb and Rose Garden features high-powered perennials that need full sun, at least 6 hours a day. The herbs and everlastings (flowers that are perfect for drying) also insist on well-drained, sandy soil. If you have clay soil, it's a good idea to build raised beds and amend the soil with lots of organic matter before planting these plants. You'll also find that the silver-leaved plants in this garden, such as silver thyme and alpine sea holly, will benefit from a mulch of coarse grit instead of organic matter.

▼ **Summer contrasts** in this garden include golden yarrow and blue-flowered globe thistle and sea holly. Roses and echinaceas add to the show.

The Planting Plan. Like spokes on a cartwheel, brick dividers separate the garden into four wedges. The wedges adjacent to the patio feature gold and scarlet plants. The other sections provide cool contrast with silver foliage and blue or purple flowers.

1 Lavender (*Lavandula angustifolia*)

2 'Silver Posie' thyme (*Thymus vulgaris* 'Silver Posie')

3 Echinacea (*Echinacea purpurea*)

4 Garden sage (*Salvia officinalis*)

5 'Taplow Blue' globe thistle (*Echinops ritro* 'Taplow Blue')

6 Alpine sea holly (*Eryngium alpinum*)

7 Artemisia (*Artemisia schmidtiana* 'Nana')

8 Lady's-mantle (*Alchemilla mollis*)

9 Golden oregano (*Origanum vulgare* 'Aureum')

10 'Scarlet Meidiland' rose (*Rosa* 'Scarlet Meidiland')

11 'Coronation Gold' yarrow (*Achillea* 'Coronation Gold')

12 Golden sage (*Salvia officinalis* 'Aurea') with Siberian squill (*Scilla siberica*)

13 Golden lemon thyme (*Thymus × citriodorus* 'Aureus')

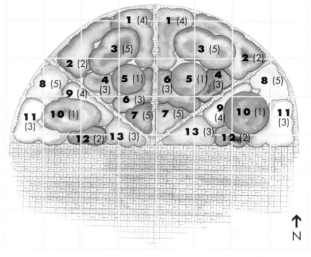

Design by Susan McClure
( ) = number of plants to plant

☐ = 65cm

↑
N

EASY-CARE ROSES, HERBS AND EVERLASTINGS This garden design features some special perennial herbs and everlasting flowers that aren't included in Part 3 of this book. But like the other easy-care perennials described there, these grow with no fuss as long as they have well-drained soil and full sun.

Alpine sea holly bears small steel-blue flowers surrounded by purple-blue bracts (modified leaves).

Golden lemon thyme, a low-grower with gold-marked foliage, has a lovely lemon scent.

Golden oregano, a creeping golden-leaved oregano, forms a handsome groundcover.

Golden sage has gold-variegated foliage and will tolerate drought.

'Scarlet Meidiland' rose is a disease-resistant ground-cover rose with arching branches up to 1 metre tall. Cut the flower in bud to dry for potpourri or wreaths. Because roses need more nourishment than herbs, provide extra compost, and fertilize and water regularly.

'Silver Posie' thyme, a small pink-flowered thyme, has grey and cream edged variegation to its leaves.

'Taplow Blue' globe thistle features globe-shaped blue flowers that reach 75cm tall. The plants have spiny thistlelike leaves.

RAISING THE GARDEN If you have an elevated patio, you'll enjoy this garden more if you raise it up to the same level. You can raise the bed by building a low semicircular retaining wall and filling the enclosed area with soil and compost.

If you don't want to fuss with laying brick to make the retaining wall and dividers for this garden, try using rot-resistant pretreated wood. If you use wooden timbers, you'll need to alter the shape of the garden. It will become a half-octagon instead of a circle.

GROWING ANNUAL EVERLASTINGS Some of the most popular and striking everlasting flowers are annuals like strawflowers rather than perennials. As long as your garden gets plenty of sun, you can substitute annual everlastings for the perennials in this garden. Keep in mind that annual everlastings need extra moisture and very fertile soil for best growth.

One of the prettiest annual everlastings is 'Pink Flamingo' cockscomb (*Celosia spicata* 'Pink Flamingo'), with feathery flower plumes that are lavender or pink at

▲ **Make a beautiful addition** to a raised patio by planting a raised bed of roses, perennials and herbs alongside it.

◀ **Use annuals** like globe amaranth to add vibrant colour to dried perennial arrangements. Grow them in full sun and very fertile soil for the best flowers.

the base fading to white at the tip. Another popular annual for dried flower crafts is globe amaranth (*Gomphrena globosa*). Its globelike flowers can be pink, violet, white, red or orange.

Strawflowers (*Bracteantha bracteata*) are a standard for dried arrangements. Their vivid daisylike flowers have petals that feel as dry as straw. They come in shades of pink, red, yellow and white. Statice (*Limonium sinuatum*) has upright spikes of papery flowers in bright blue, pink, purple, yellow or white.

EASY-CARE ROSES Roses are wonderful companions for perennials and herbs – just be sure you choose roses that are easy to care for! You can start with old-fashioned roses such as fragrant gallicas like 'Camaieux', and Damask roses like 'Madame Hardy'. These roses are hardy and resistant to diseases, but they bloom primarily in early summer. Even better are newer hybrid shrub roses that bloom repeatedly through summer and autumn. Here are some of the best:
'The Fairy' bears many small pink flowers in summer and autumn, and forms a neat mound about 1 metre tall and wide.
Meidiland roses are groundcover roses that bloom heavily in late spring, and then rebloom in summer

and autumn. White 'Snow Carpet' grows as a groundcover to 30cm tall. 'Scarlet Meidiland' reaches 1 metre tall and spreads up to 2 metres wide.
Rugosa rose (*R. rugosa*) is tough, disease-resistant, and salt-tolerant. It grows into a large shrub, 1 to 2 metres tall, with pink, white, or red flowers in late spring and summer.
'Sea Foam' has pink buds and fragrant white flowers in early summer, and reblooms almost continuously for the rest of the growing season. It grows to 30cm tall and can spread up to 100cm wide.

To get the best from easy-care roses, plant them in rich and moist but well-drained soil in full sun. Fertilize in spring and summer with a balanced organic fertilizer. Prune off dead, damaged or diseased branches whenever you find them. Water as needed to keep the soil evenly moist.

You can cut rosebuds for drying when they are coloured but still closed. They make a wonderful addition to potpourri. Some roses produce tart, berrylike rose hips that are rich in vitamin C and make a good ingredient in herb teas. Harvest rose hips when they are bright red, dry them for several weeks and then grind or crush them for teas.

DRYING FLOWERS AND HERBS To enjoy the beauty and colour of your perennial, herb and rose garden year-round, plan on cutting and drying some of its bounty of flowers and colourful foliage. Harvest flowers for drying when they are young, fresh and showing perfect colour. A great time to harvest is midmorning, after dew has dried off the petals.

Herbs and everlasting flowers usually dry well in a warm, dark, ventilated room or shed, and can be stored in a firm-sided plastic storage box. Other flowers need to be covered with a drying agent like silica gel for best results.

Upright Drying. Dry large or full flowers like yarrow upright so they maintain their open shape. Gather small bunches of stems and set them upright in dry vases or put individual stems in a drying rack. To make your own drying rack, cut holes in the sides of a cardboard box and set a wire mesh screen on top. Stick stems of perennial flowers through the screen to dry upright.

After the flower petals dry, lay the stems on a table in a well-ventilated room to finish drying.

Dangle Drying. Plants with narrow stems like lavender dry well if you bundle them and hang them in a well-ventilated room or attic (their colours may stay brighter if you keep them in a dark spot).

Harvest flower stems and leafy sprigs. Make sure each piece you harvest has at least 10cm of stem. Hang the stems to dry in bundles of up to 1cm thick, and hold each bundle together with a twist tie. If humidity is high, make the bundles smaller. Thick-stemmed flowers such as astilbes or Michaelmas daisies should be left to dry individually. Dangle the bundles or individual stems from a drying rack or coat hanger and leave them to dry.

Drying with Silica Gel. Silica gel works well for drying thick succulent flowers like peonies and rosebuds. Do not treat edible flowers or herbs you want to use for cooking with silica gel.

Harvest flower buds and newly opened flowers. Remove the stems or strip off the leaves. Put a 2-cm layer of silica gel in the bottom of a plastic container that has an airtight lid. Set individual flowers in it, placing them so they don't touch.

Work additional silica gel around the petals, then cover the flowers completely. Layer in more flowers and silica gel until the container is full and seal it. Leave the flowers stored in the silica gel until you're ready to use them.

▶ **Plants dry** well hanging in a well-ventilated room. Keeping them in a dark place may help to preserve their colours.

MAKING A SIMPLE WREATH

Once you have a collection of dried flowers and herbs, don't let them sit in boxes. You can easily turn them into a lovely wreath to hang on your kitchen door or living room wall. It will lift your spirits and remind you on chilly winter days that another gardening season is just a few short months away.

You will need:

- Dried flowers, petals and leaves, dried herbs
- A straw or grass wreath base
- Clear, quick-setting glue or a hot glue gun
- 25-cm length of medium-gauge florist's wire
- Ribbon

1 Gather your materials on a table or work area. Choose ribbon that complements the colours of the dried flowers and herbs.

2 Spread a thick layer of glue on a small area of the wreath base. Make sure the glue spreads into the nooks and crannies of the wreath surface.

▶ **A herb and everlasting wreath** makes a beautiful and fragrant keepsake of your perennial, herb, and rose garden.

3 Press the petals and leaves firmly onto the glue. Then spread glue on another section of the wreath and press on more dried material. Repeat until the sides and top surface of the wreath are covered.

4 Gather a bunch of dried herbs and flowers and cut the stems short. Wrap the piece of wire around the stems, then tie the ribbon around the bunch and make a bow. Push the ends of the wire into the wreath base to fasten the bunch in place.

A COLONIAL COTTAGE GARDEN

*Cottage gardens have been around since the Middle Ages,
but they're still the freshest, most fun gardening style around.*

In a cottage garden, anything goes. Originally, gardeners grew vegetables, herbs, flowers, and even fruit trees together in their cottage gardens. By Victorian times, the cottage garden had become a fragrant, colourful mix of heirloom flowers and prized varieties.

A cottage garden is a very informal garden. Plants spread and mingle, creating a rich mix of colours and textures. The natural combinations are beautiful, but to get the most from your garden, you'll need to enforce a little organization. This design mixes cottage garden plants with a colonial garden layout. The design holds the plants firmly in check with a picket fence and brick or stone pathways that divide the garden into four beds. The pathways between beds and stepping-stones in the beds offer easy access whenever you need to plunge in and cut back or divide a spreading perennial that threatens to swamp its neighbours. They also let you wander in all parts of the garden, inviting you to admire its beauty and fragrance up close or to cut a bouquet of fresh flowers.

▼ **Lavender and 'Heritage' roses** fill the Colonial Cottage Garden with colour and fragrance in early summer. Bugle, Siberian iris, and peonies also add their lovely flowers to this charming setting.

The Planting Plan. The garden starts with a framework of roses, hydrangeas, and easy-care perennials, including lavender, daylilies, anemones, violets, bugle, and spring bulbs. You give the design your unique style by filling in the framework with your choices of plants from "Perennials for Your Sunny Cottage Garden." You'll need to make your own decisions regarding the number of each type to plant. See "How Many Perennials Should You Buy?" on page 67 for guidance. When you plant these beds, put the shortest plants next to the paths, then place other plants by height, building to the showstopper perennials in the centre.

Design by Susan McClure
☐ = 1 metre
↑ N

1 'Heritage' rose (*Rosa* 'Heritage')

2 Japanese anemone (*Anemone × hybrida*)

3 'Forever Pink' hydrangea (*Hydrangea macrophylla* 'Forever Pink')

4 Showstopper plants

5 Edging plants

6 Lavender (*Lavandula angustifolia*)

7 Daylilies (*Hemerocallis*) with daffodils (*Narcissus*)

8 'Blaauw' juniper (*Juniperus chinensis* 'Blaauw')

9 Medium-height plants

10 Siberian iris (*Iris sibirica*)

11 Labrador violet (*Viola labradorica*) with *Tulipa tarda* and bugle (*Ajuga*)

PERENNIALS FOR YOUR SUNNY COTTAGE GARDEN

The lists below separate easy-care perennials and bulbs into categories so it's easy to see where they can fit into the Colonial Cottage Garden. To give your garden a more restful, designed look, plant clumps of three or more of each plant together and repeat plantings of the same plant in two or more beds. You'll find more information about how to grow each of the plants in Part 3 of this book.

Edging Plants	**Medium-Height Plants**	**Showstopper Plants**
Achillea tomentosa (Woolly yarrow)	*Anemone sylvestris* (Snowdrop anemone)	*Baptisia australis* (Blue false indigo)
Alchemilla mollis (Lady's-mantle)	*Asclepias tuberosa* (Butterfly weed)	*Coreopsis* (Tickseed)
Anemone blanda (Windflower)	*Geranium* (Cranesbills, Hardy geraniums)	*Echinacea purpurea*
Armeria maritima (Thrift)	*Heuchera sanguinea* (Coral bells)	*Hemerocallis* (Daylilies)
Artemisia schmidtiana 'Nana'	*Lavandula angustifolia* 'Jean Davis' ('Jean Davis' lavender)	*Iris sibirica* (Siberian iris)
Crocus (Crocuses)	*Narcissus* (Daffodils)	*Phlox maculata* (Meadow phlox)
Eranthis hyemalis (Winter aconite)	*Paeonia officinalis* (Common peony)	*Platycodon grandiflorus* (Balloon flower)
Muscari (Grape hyacinths)	*Rudbeckia fulgida* var. *sullivantii* 'Goldsturm'	
Narcissus jonquilla (Jonquil)	*Salvia nemorosa* 'Ostfriesland' (Salvia 'East Friesland')	
Pulsatilla vulgaris (Pasqueflower)	*Scabiosa caucasica* (Pincushion flower, Scabious)	
Scilla siberica (Siberian squill)	*Stokesia laevis* (Stokes' aster)	
Tulipa greigii		
Verbena corymbosa		

▶ **In an informal cottage garden,** perennials cheerfully mix and mingle. There's no limit to the combinations of colours and textures you can create.

PERSONALIZING THE GARDEN In your cottage garden, you can grow cherished passalong plants from your grandmother's garden, a mix of flowers and herbs, old-fashioned flowers, the latest varieties – or all of the above. A cottage garden is *your* garden in the truest sense of the word: It can be whatever you want to make it. You should feel free to add personal favourite plants, even if they're not in the lists on the preceding page; just place them according to their height.

For a truly cheerful cottage garden look, be sure to include plenty of spring-flowering bulbs between clumps of perennials. Mixing perennials and bulbs has two big pluses. First, the early-blooming bulbs add colour in spring, when your perennials are just getting started. Then, when the bulb show ends, the perennial foliage and flowers hide the bulb foliage as it ages and yellows.

Cottage gardens traditionally include old-fashioned flowers such as honeysuckle, sweet peas, columbines (*Aquilegia*), foxgloves, bearded iris, poppies, pansies, and pinks. These plants may not meet an easy-care standard because they need special treatment or are prone to pest problems. However, you may still want to include some of them in your garden to lend it a distinct cottage garden air.

Here are some hints to help you find those special plants that make your cottage garden uniquely your own:

● Seek out a specialty nursery that features old-fashioned or unusual flowers for cutting, fragrance, or drying.

● If your grandparents or other older relatives decide to sell their home, transplant some of their favourite flowers to your garden when they move, and start a family tradition.

● Splurge when spring fever hits. Go ahead and buy that perennial you've been admiring in a mail-order catalogue.

● Visit a gardening friend, and ask for a division or cutting of one of her prize plants.

● Pick your favourite era in history – Victorian, Colonial, Elizabethan, or whatever – and grow some of its most popular plants in your garden.

When you've dug plants or taken divisions or cuttings from someone else's garden, check for pest or disease problems before you add the plants to your garden. Take a close look at the tops and undersides of the leaves. Look for insects and insect eggs, or misshapen and discoloured leaves. Check the roots and crowns for signs of rot. If you find symptoms, don't keep the plant – put it in a sealed plastic bag and throw it away.

If you're trying out an unfamiliar plant, ask the person who gave it to you how tall it will grow, so you know where to position it in your garden. (You can also find this information in a catalogue or gardening encyclopedia.) Check whether it will spread rapidly, and whether it's prone to pest or disease problems. You may decide it's not right for your garden after all. If the plant fits in, however, you'll find that you get twice the enjoyment from it – first, because it's lovely, and second, because you have a special relationship with it.

CREATING A SMALLER GARDEN If you'd like a garden that's smaller than the one shown in the plan, you can easily cut it down to size. Simply plant two sections of the garden on either side of your front door. You can still surround it with a picket fence, or just use a pathway to enclose it. Make sure the tallest flowers won't cover up your windows or doors. Modify the access paths so they branch off from the path near your front step or entry.

PLANTING ON A SHADY SITE If your site is in dappled sun or light shade (receiving about four hours of sun a day), you can use the Colonial Cottage Garden design with shade-tolerant perennials instead of perennials for full sun. In a lightly shaded site, the basic framework might include edgings of fragrant violets and lily-of-the-valley. Medium-height plants could include snowdrop anemones, bleeding hearts, and coral bells. Substitute hydrangeas or shrubby honeysuckles, which tolerate light shade, for the sun-loving roses, and plant astilbes instead of lavender. Then add other shade-tolerant easy-care perennials as you please, according to height. And remember to tuck in plenty of spring bulbs for early colour!

PERENNIALS FOR A LIGHTLY SHADED COTTAGE GARDEN Try these cottage garden plants in a lightly shaded site that gets at least four hours of sun a day. They're arranged by height so you can see where they can fit into the garden. Plant clumps of three or more of each together and repeat plantings of the same plant in two or more beds. There is more information about how to grow each of these plants in Part 3 of this book.

Edging Plants	*Tulipa greigii*
Alchemilla (Lady's-mantle)	
Ajuga (Bugles)	**Medium-Height Plants**
Anemone blanda (Windflower)	*Anemone sylvestris* (Snowdrop anemone)
Asarum canadense (Canadian wild ginger, Canadian snakeroot)	*Astilbe × arendsii* 'Bratschleier' ('Bridal Veil' astilbe)
Brunnera macrophylla	*Dicentra formosa* (Bleeding hearts)
Convallaria majalis (Lily-of-the-valley)	*Geranium* (Cranesbills, Hardy geraniums)
Corydalis lutea (Yellow corydalis)	*Helleborus orientalis* (Lenten rose)
Crocus (Crocuses)	*Heuchera* (Coral bells)
Epimedium (Epimediums)	*Hosta fortunei* (Hostas)
Eranthis hyemalis (Winter aconite)	*Mertensia pulmonarioides* (Virginian cowslips)
Geranium sanguineum (Bloody cranesbill)	*Narcissus* (Daffodils)
Muscari (Grape hyacinths)	**Showstopper Plants**
Phlox divaricata (Blue phlox)	*Astilbe × arendsii* 'Cattleya' ('Cattleya' astilbe)
Pulmonaria (Lungworts)	*Hemerocallis* (Daylilies)
Sanguinaria canadensis (Bloodroot)	*Hosta ventricosa* (Blue-leaved hosta)
Scilla siberica (Siberian squill)	*Iris sibirica* (Siberian iris)
Tiarella cordifolia (Foamflowers)	*Mentha × piperita* (Peppermint)

COTTAGE GARDEN LORE Cottage garden plants are rich in history, hidden meanings, and mythical stories. This heritage makes your garden more than just a place to grow plants; it lets you bring the past to life. For example, plants played important roles in some ancient myths. And in Victorian times, people gave bouquets containing plants with special meanings as a way of passing messages. Choosing plants with a theme from folklore or history will make it even more fun to show friends and family around your garden. Time-travel now as you decide which plants to feature in your cottage garden.

Magical Plants

Tulips. The most lovely, fragrant, and long-lasting of the tulips are probably inhabited by pixies and their families, says old English lore. Check carefully before you dig these charmed bulbs up so you don't provoke pixie wrath.

Yarrow. Sturdy, aromatic yarrow once steeped in kettles of witches' brew. It's also an old-time remedy for soothing bloody noses and sores. Both uses led to the practice of hanging yarrow in a work shed, where it would magically repel thieves and be handy for treating cuts or scrapes. Although the magic may have gone out of yarrow, it still makes a fine cut flower.

▲ Yarrow

Flowers of Folklore and Myth

Anemones. Flexible-stemmed anemone flowers have long been linked to wind. An age-old question is whether a gentle breeze coaxes these windflowers to open as the stems bend and move. Ancient Greeks believed windflowers arose from the goddess Venus' tears, so anemones have long represented pain, suffering, and forsaken friends.

▲ Anemones

Daffodils. Sunny daffodils came by their botanical name of *Narcissus* from the myth of Narcissus, a Greek youth so handsome and vain that he fell in love with his reflection and took his own life in frustration. Where his blood fell, the first *Narcissus* sprang up.

Lily-of-the-valley. Irish lore claimed that fairies climbed lily-of-the-valley flowers like ladders. In Korea, the sword-shaped leaves were said to have arisen from drops of blood shed by a dragon-fighting giant.

Peony. The peony has a mixed folklore heritage. Ancient Greeks enjoyed it, finding magic in the glow of its moonlit flowers. Later Victorian sentimentalists, however, chastised the peony. To them, it meant anger and shame because of the blush of pink or red-flowered varieties.

Siberian irises. Siberian irises come in a sparkling spectrum of colours – blues, purples, yellows, white, and red – justifying its connection to Iris, Greek goddess of the rainbow. The iris assumed a royal lineage when it became part of Louis VII's coat of arms in twelfth-century France.

Flowers with Special Symbolism

Lavender. Lavender, an herb with a wonderful aroma, became a symbol of distrust in Victorian times. Perhaps the distrust is on the part of clothes moths and other pests that avoid sprigs set in dresser drawers! On a happier note, other early herbalists quilted lavender into a nightcap to set the mind at ease and encourage memory.

Lily-of-the-valley. The delicate but deliciously scented floral bells of lily-of-the-valley raised romantic notions of returning happiness in Victorian times.

▲ Tulips

Tulips. Tulips were the cause of rampant speculation and financial ruin in sixteenth-century Europe. But by Victorian times, tulips had been forgiven and had taken on the meaning "I love you".

Violets. Petite violets represented modesty in Victorian times, giving rise to the phrase "shrinking violet".

Useful Plants of Yesteryear

Iris. Roots of aromatic iris species have a rich violet aroma and have been used for fragrance or medicine since the time of the ancient Greeks. Today they flavour toothpaste and scent perfume.

Southernwood. The scented leaves of southernwood (*Artemisia abrotanum*) were used in folk medicine and treasured for keeping clean laundry smelling fresh (try it – it works!).

Violets. Violet petals, candied for desserts today as well as in historic times, were long reputed to soothe sore throats and coughs.

KEEPING YOUR COTTAGE GARDEN MANAGEABLE

After a season or two, some of the plants in your cottage garden may have spread too rambunctiously to suit you. That's when it's time to divide large clumps, thin overcrowded seedlings, remove plants growing in the wrong places, or open up space for new plants. When cutting back creeping plants, remove both the tops and roots. Be especially thorough with aggressive spreaders, such as mints or ajugas. They can resprout from even tiny sections of root. If you work when the soil is moist, you may be able to uproot small plants just by grasping the base of the stem and pulling gently. But if the soil is hard or the plant is large, don't rely on hand-pulling. Use a small spade to dig around the plant or section of plant you want to remove and lever out a large ball of roots and soil. (For more on keeping spreading perennials under control, see page 116.)

To limit the spread of self-sowing perennials such as verbena, echinaceas, and phlox, cut off the flowers as soon as they fade. If you want a few new seedlings, let one or two flowers mature and spread seeds. Uproot unwanted seedlings with a hoe, scraping the soil surface often when it's moist. To discourage new seeds from germinating, cover the soil with a layer of newspaper covered with organic mulch.

A DYNAMIC DRIVEWAY BORDER

Welcome everyone who enters your driveway with a bold border of easy-care perennials. Planting perennials along the driveway changes a necessary but unattractive feature of your front garden into a terrific asset.

In the Dynamic Driveway Border, big clumps of ornamental grasses form the backbone of the garden, set off by groups of gold, pink, and white perennial flowers. The garden begins with low plants near the street, so you'll have a clear view of oncoming traffic when you pull out of the driveway. Then it builds in height with a mix of grasses, a rugosa rose, and bright perennials. As you pass by, the border gives the effect of a billowing field of changing colour and texture.

▶ **In the early spring,** this border features bright yellow winter aconites, pink and white Spanish bluebells, and yellow and white crocuses.

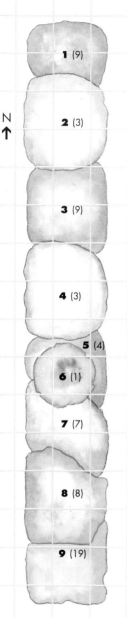

Design by Bobbie Schwartz
( ) = number of plants to plant

☐ = 1 metre

The Planting Plan. Many of the tall perennials in this border don't need staking as long as they have plenty of sun and moderately fertile soil. Some, like miscanthus grass, will need simple grow-through supports. Set wire-grid supports over the plants in spring; they will grow through the grid and hide it from view. Leave the dried foliage of the grasses in place for winter interest; cut back their dried stems 10 to 15cm above soil level in early spring. One long side of the Dynamic Driveway Border abuts the lawn. Edge it with a barrier to prevent lawn grasses from invading the bed.

1 'Herbstsonne' coneflower (*Rudbeckia* 'Herbstsonne') with pink Spanish bluebells (*Hyacinthoides hispanicus* 'Rose') and late-blooming yellow daffodils (*Narcissus*)

2 Miscanthus grass (*Miscanthus sinensis* 'Strictus') with late-blooming bicolour daffodils and white Spanish bluebells

3 'Fujiyama' phlox (*Phlox paniculata* 'Fujiyama') with *Tulipa pulchella* 'Persian Pearl'

4 'Adagio' miscanthus (*Miscanthus sinensis* 'Adagio') with midseason yellow daffodils and yellow crocuses (*Crocus*)

5 'Biokovo' cranesbill (*Geranium* × *cantabrigiense* 'Biokovo')

6 'Scabrosa' rugosa rose (*Rosa* 'Scabrosa')

7 'Karl Foerster' feather reed grass (*Calamagrostis* × *acutiflora* 'Karl Foerster') with midseason bicolour daffodils and white crocuses

8 'Moonbeam' coreopsis (*Coreopsis verticillata* 'Moonbeam') with winter aconite (*Eranthis hyemalis*)

9 'Bees' Ruby' thrift (*Armeria* 'Bees' Ruby')

▶ **As autumn arrives,** 'Herbstsonne' coneflowers, coreopsis, and rugosa rose continue blooming strongly. The rippling plumes of the ornamental grasses fill the border with intriguing sights and sounds.

 **A Dynamic Driveway Border**

GARDENS FOR SHORT AND LONG DRIVEWAYS The Dynamic Driveway Border is designed for a 15-metre driveway, but chances are your driveway isn't precisely 15 metres. If it's shorter, adapt the plan by planting fewer plants of each type. For example, cut back the number of phlox and coreopsis from nine to seven or five. Keep in mind that odd numbers of plants in each clump tend to produce a more natural look. That's because when you plant an even number of plants, you'll be tempted to set them in formal squares or rectangles that won't look right with this design.

To extend the border for a longer driveway, repeat some of the groups of perennials. You might, for instance, expand the midsection of the border – repeating the 'Karl Foerster' feather reed grass, 'Biokovo' cranesbill, rugosa rose, and the miscanthus grass sequence to add an extra 6 metres. Or, you can expand the size of each cluster of perennials. Instead of using only nine 'Moonbeam' coreopsis or 'Fujiyama' phlox, enlarge that planting to 11 or 13. To add a metre with a single plant, add another large *Miscanthus*.

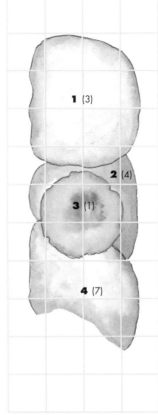

EXTEND THE BORDER
For a longer driveway you can repeat the midsection of the border to add an extra 6 metres.

1 'Adagio' miscanthus (*Miscanthus sinensis* 'Adagio') with midseason yellow daffodils and yellow crocuses (*Crocus*)

2 'Biokovo' cranesbill (*Geranium* × *cantabrigiense* 'Biokovo')

3 'Scabrosa' rugosa rose (*Rosa* 'Scabrosa')

4 'Karl Foerster' feather reed grass (*Calamagrostis* × *acutiflora* 'Karl Foerster') with midseason bicolour daffodils and white crocuses

▶ **A wooden fence** edged with a groundcover makes a nice border for a rural driveway. Plant tall perennials like blue false indigo behind the fence for added interest.

CREATING A WIDE BORDER If you'd like even more of a good thing, you can expand the Dynamic Driveway Border from 2 to 3 metres wide. This allows you to add another layer of low-growing perennials all along the edges of the driveway. Here are some ideas to try:

● Move the tall 'Herbstsonne' coneflowers back and plant a salvia in the foreground.

● Plant thrift (*Armeria maritima*) in front of the 'Fujiyama' phlox and add another rugosa rose in the background.

● Move the rugosa rose back, set 'Moonbeam' coreopsis at its feet, and add more 'Biokovo' cranesbill as an edging.

● Beside the street, use blue salvia behind sweeps of thrift and 'Moonbeam' coreopsis.

PLANTING ALONG A SHADY DRIVEWAY If you have shade trees planted alongside your driveway, the Dynamic Driveway Border just won't work for your site. But you can perk up a row of trees—and cut down on tricky mowing—by planting perennial groundcovers under the trees right up to the edge of

◀ **Soften the edge** of a driveway or path by planting sweeps of graceful perennials like this salvia alongside.

the driveway. Bugles (*Ajuga*) and epimediums (*Epimedium*) are both good choices. Try interplanting ferns or spring bulbs for added colour and texture.

◀ **Mix hostas** with variegated leaves and different leaf colours to make a distinctive edging for a shady driveway.

GREETING GARDENS If you're not ready to plunge into planting a border to span your entire driveway, try planting a smaller "greeting garden" instead. By carefully choosing a small group of easy-care perennials, you can create a charming garden that will brighten the entrance of your driveway or a spot by your front door all season long.

◀ A Shady Hosta Garden

Here's a chance to plant your favourite hosta, or a great excuse to buy a special new cultivar you've been longing for! The handsome hosta foliage is a season-long central feature of this grouping. The Solomon's seal and Jerusalem sage foliage will also be an asset from spring through to autumn, as well as provide a lovely show of spring flowers.

- Squills (*Scilla*)
- 'Mrs. Moon' Jerusalem sage (*Pulmonaria saccharata* 'Mrs. Moon')
- Hosta (*Hosta* species or cultivar)
- Variegated Solomon's seal (*Polygonatum odoratum* 'Variegatum')

▶ A Shady Garden with Ferns

The delicate flowers of violets and foamflowers look cool and inviting in this elegant grouping. The silver-flecked leaves of the Japanese painted fern are lovely from spring through to autumn, while the black snakeroot flower spikes add a dramatic touch in summer.

- Violets (*Viola*)
- Foamflowers (*Tiarella*)
- Japanese painted fern (*Athyrium niponicum* 'Pictum')
- Black snakeroot (*Cimicifuga racemosa*)

◀ A Silvery Sunny Garden

This quartet proves that you don't need a fancy plant list for a great garden. The arching stems of Russian sage and gorgeous silvery artemisia foliage make this garden a pleasure to view all season long. Grape hyacinths provide spring cheer and then go dormant. Airy blue flower sprays of Russian sage bloom in summer, and bold royal purple New England asters follow in the autumn.

- Grape hyacinths
  (*Muscari*)
- 'Nana' artemisia (*Artemisia schmidtiana* 'Nana')
- Russian sage
  (*Perovskia atriplicifolia*)
- 'Purple Dome' New England aster
  (*Aster novae-angliae* 'Purple Dome')

▶ A Multicoloured Sunny Garden

Daffodils and blue bugle flowers get this minigarden off to a great spring start. Coreopsis, *Aster x frickartii*, and iris supply the summer colour. After the iris flowers fade, its spiky leaves add interest into autumn, while the coreopsis and aster keep right on blooming. And throughout the season, crinkled, glossy bugle foliage is an eye-catching accent.

- Assorted daffodils
  (five or seven bulbs of each cultivar)
  (*Narcissus*)
- 'Metallica Crispa' bugle (*Ajuga pyramidalis* 'Metallica Crispa')
- 'Moonbeam' coreopsis
  (*Coreopsis verticillata* 'Moonbeam')
- Frikart's aster
  (*Aster* x *frikartii*)
- Blue or purple Siberian iris
  (*Iris sibirica*)

A Fabulous Four-Season Garden

An inviting garden at your front door offers a wonderful welcome to guests.
It also gives you and your family a pleasant and colourful view to enjoy every day.

Don't let stodgy evergreens surround your entryway! Use perennials to say a cheerful hello and create a beautiful scene all year long.

This contemporary entryway garden for a lightly shaded site features a path leading past blocks of perennials that combine handsome foliage and flowers for great year-round colour and interest. On the opposite side of the path, a mixed planting of shrubs and perennials gives the scene greater impact and extra off-season colour and interest.

▼ **In the spring,** the Fabulous Four-Season Garden features white foamflowers, Lenten roses, tulips interplanted with bleeding heart, yellow corydalis, and the lovely blossoms of amelanchier.

The Planting Plan. The square-grid planting system used for this design makes the garden extra-easy to plant and tend. Self-sown corydalis seedlings will pop up in neighbouring squares; watch for them and pull them out before they get too weedy. Prune any dead or broken branches from the woody plants as needed to keep them healthy and attractive. For the pots of annuals, use yellow coleus, fuchsia, and pink impatiens.

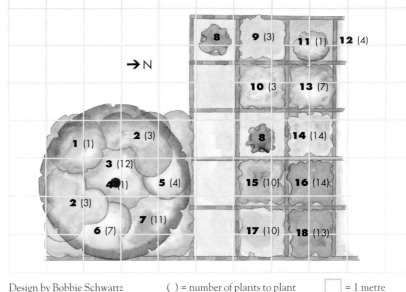

→ N

Design by Bobbie Schwartz   ( ) = number of plants to plant   ☐ = 1 metre

1 Oakleaf hydrangea (*Hydrangea quercifolia*)

2 'Scarletta' leucothoe (*Leucothoe* 'Scarletta')

3 'Sulphureum' epimedium (*Epimedium × versicolour* 'Sulphureum')

4 Amelanchier, serviceberry (*Amelanchier canadensis*)

5 'Hyperion' daylily (*Hemerocallis* 'Hyperion')

6 Lady's-mantle (*Alchemilla mollis*)

7 Astilbe (*Astilbe chinensis* var. *pumila*) with winter aconite (*Eranthis hyemalis*)

8 Potted annuals

9 Christmas rose (*Helleborus niger*) with golden crocus (*Crocus chrysanthus*)

10 Lenten rose (*Helleborus orientalis*)

11 'Krossa Regal' hosta (*Hosta* 'Krossa Regal') with trumpet daffodil (*Narcissus* 'Dutch Master' and others) and Siberian squill (*Scilla siberica*)

12 'Professor van der Weilen' astilbe (*Astilbe thunbergii* 'Professor van der Weilen') with 'Silver Chimes' daffodil (*Narcissus* 'Silver Chimes')

13 Foamflower (*Tiarella cordifolia*)

14 Yellow corydalis (*Corydalis lutea*)

15 'Palace Purple' heuchera (*Heuchera micrantha* var. *diversifolia* 'Palace Purple')

16 'Fuji Blue' balloon flower (*Platycodon grandiflorus* 'Fuji Blue') with Spanish bluebells (*Hyacinthoides hispanicus*)

17 Cranesbill (*Geranium renardii*)

18 Wild bleeding heart (*Dicentra formosa*) with 'Lilac Wonder' tulip (*Tulipa saxatilis* 'Lilac Wonder')

◄ **Foliage colours** and textures are the main features of interest in the fall garden. Oakleaf hydrangea blossoms and the red foliage of the amelanchier are highlights.

A SUNNY ENTRYWAY GARDEN If your entryway garden faces to the south, it is probably in full sun all day. You can adapt the Fabulous Four-Season Garden to your site by planting sun-loving perennials in place of the shade-loving perennials in the design. Just use the list below with the planting plan shown on page 65.

1 Oakleaf hydrangea (*Hydrangea quercifolia*)

2 'Scarletta' leucothoe (*Leucothoe* 'Scarletta')

3 'Sulphureum' epimedium (*Epimedium* × *versicolour* 'Sulphureum')

4 Amelanchier, serviceberry (*Amelanchier canadensis*)

5 'Hyperion' daylily (*Hemerocallis* 'Hyperion')

6 Lady's-mantle (*Alchemilla mollis*)

7 Astilbe (*Astilbe chinensis* var. *pumila*) with winter aconite (*Eranthis hyemalis*)

8 Potted annuals

9 Adam's-needle (*Yucca filamentosa*) with golden crocus (*Crocus chrysanthus*)

10 'Autumn Joy' sedum (*Sedum* 'Herbstfreude')

11 'Krossa Regal' hosta (*Hosta* 'Krossa Regal') with trumpet daffodil (*Narcissus* 'Dutch Master' and others) and Siberian squill (*Scilla siberica*)

12 Russian sage *Perovskia atriplicifolia*) with 'Silver Chimes' daffodil (*Narcissus* 'Silver Chimes'

13 'Album' bloody cranesbill (*Geranium sanguineum* 'Album')

14 'Moonbeam' coreopsis (*Coreopsis verticillata* 'Moonbeam')

15 'Palace Purple' heuchera (*Heuchera micrantha* var. *diversifolia* 'Palace Purple')

16 'Fuji Blue' balloon flower (*Platycodon grandiflorus* 'Fuji Blue') with Spanish bluebells (*Hyacinthoides hispanicus*)

17 Cranesbill (*Geranium renardii*)

18 Pink tickseed (*Coreopsis rosea*) with 'Lilac Wonder' tulip (*Tulipa saxatilis* 'Lilac Wonder')

▶ **'Golden Sword'** Adam's needle (*Yucca flaccida* 'Golden Sword') is a bold accent plant for a four-season garden in a sunny location.

Changing the Layout. Many houses don't have a corner nook like the one shown in the Fabulous Four-Season Garden. However, you can adapt the garden to suit almost any house shape. Here, for example, the garden around the amelanchier is planted to the right of the perennials along the pathway, providing a lovely backdrop that frames the perennials like a picture. If you have a shady site, use this layout with the plant list on page 53; if your site is sunny, refer to the list of plants on page 54 instead.

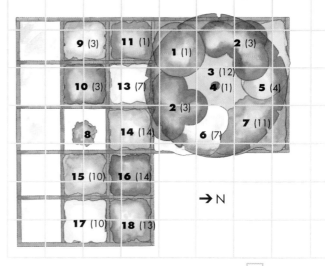

( ) = number of plants to plant   ☐ = 1 metre

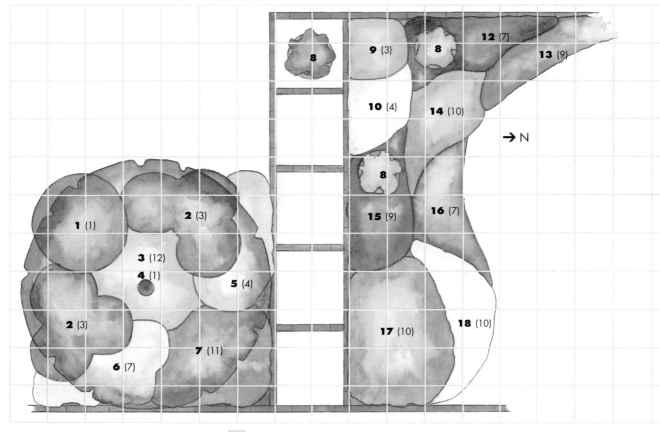

( ) = number of plants to plant   ☐ = 35cm

A Casual Entry Garden. The block layout of the Fabulous Four-Season Garden may not match all house styles. And if you prefer informal gardens, it just may not match *you*! For a more relaxed approach, change the planting grid to a gentle S-curve bed as shown here. If you have a shady site, use this layout with the plant list on page 53; if your site is sunny, refer to the list of plants on page 54 instead.

USING GARDEN ART FOR FOUR-SEASON INTEREST It's not easy to create a four-season garden with perennials alone, because most of them die back or get cut back as winter approaches. Woody plants like shrubs and trees offer winter interest with colourful bark or their branch pattern. But if you don't have space to plant trees or shrubs, or want an instant effect, try garden art for year-round interest. While not "natural," sculpture and gardens work well together and are fun too!

Garden art is very popular, so you're bound to find something that suits your taste and budget. Animal or wildlife statues are naturals for gardens. If you like an old-fashioned look, consider antiques such as old water pumps, wagon wheels, or ceramic planters. Sundials and pedestal-mounted gazing balls are classic options. For contemporary gardens, look for modern art such as stone or metal sculptures.

▲ **A birdbath is a sure source of** year-round interest, because it will attract a variety of birds to your garden in every season.

A birdbath in a strategic spot is a great garden ornament that will bring the magic of birds to any garden. Bright white birdbaths stand out, demanding immediate attention. Darker colours are more subtle; they draw the eye more gently, without being so much of a feature in their own right.

Place outdoor art and other garden structures in a prominent place. A garden statue at the back of a perennial garden draws you to look across all the layers of the garden. Or try yard art in sitting areas, or at the junction of two walks, or in a niche beside a wall.

When using a garden statue in the perennial garden, be sure to select a statue that's tall enough to rise above the perennials (which can hide the base), or set it on blocks or an upside-down pot to give it some extra height.

▲ **A sundial** is a classic garden ornament and seems particularly appropriate for a four-season garden, marking the hours throughout the year.

◀ **Birdhouses serve a practical purpose** in your garden – attracting birds that may help control insect pests – but they also add an artistic or whimsical touch .

5 MORE FOUR-SEASON INTEREST TRICKS Look for ways to add four-season interest in every part of your garden, not just in your perennial borders. Here are some ideas that will boost your garden's looks year-round.

● Set up a trellis between two areas of your garden that you'd like to keep separate. It's a friendly way to separate the children's play area, for example, from a quiet reading area. Plant clematis or another flowering climber to thread through the trellis for in-season colour, and choose a trellis with a woven lattice or other geometric structure for winter interest.

● Add garden furniture that can withstand the elements through the winter. A classic wooden bench is the ideal accent for a natural garden. Wrought iron furniture fits an old-fashioned garden. For a contemporary garden in mild climates, simple white plastic tables and chairs provide bold relief to a green lawn or shady sitting area.

● Create living lawn art by setting a showy potted tender perennial into a large, attractive container. In the winter, take the plant indoors and fill the container with evergreen branches.

● Highlight the form of a weeping cherry or other decorative tree with garden lights that silhouette the tree at night.

● Put a handsome gazebo near the edge of your property and surround it with perennials. It will be a favourite sitting spot in summer, giving you pleasant memories when you look out from inside your house on a chilly winter day.

Easy-Care Basics

For a great perennial garden, it pays to understand the basic gardening techniques that will help your easy-care perennials get a strong start and live long, healthy lives.

The place to start is your soil. In "Soil Care for Beautiful Perennial Gardens", you'll learn about the different kinds of soil and how they affect plant growth. You'll discover the small miracles that can happen when you add organic matter to your soil. You'll also learn how to make your own compost and use mulch to build your soil's organic matter content.

In "Buying and Planting Perennials", you'll find out where and how to buy quality perennials. There are guidelines for deciding how many perennials to buy when you're planting a garden you've designed yourself. You'll also learn the ins and outs of planting perennials both large and small.

The "Perennial Care Primer" includes how-to instructions for efficient watering. You'll find helpful hints for using soaker hoses and drip irrigation systems. There's plenty of useful information on the best organic fertilizers for perennials. You'll also learn how to stake unobtrusively, revive perennials by dividing, and keep ahead of weeds.

While pests and diseases aren't big problems when you grow easy-care perennials (that's one of the reasons we like them so much!), you can help to discourage any problems by browsing through the tips and techniques covered in the "Perennial Problem Solver". You'll also find helpful hints for preventing deer and other animal pests from feeding on your perennials.

SOIL CARE FOR BEAUTIFUL PERENNIAL GARDENS

Great soil care is the true secret of easy-care perennial gardening. After all, the soil is the source of moisture and nutrients your plants need to thrive. And the soil protects the roots and crowns of your perennials. The best time for improving your soil is in the autumn. The weather is pleasant, and it's generally a less busy gardening season than spring. So take time to add amendments and work the soil on sunny autumn afternoons. Your autumn labours will pay great spring dividends – loose, rich soil ready for planting all your wonderful new perennials.

LEARN ABOUT YOUR SOIL

The first question to answer about your soil is: What kind of soil do you have? There are three basic types of soil: sandy, clay, and loamy. To identify your soil's type, stick your hand in the soil and rub some of it between your fingers.

If it feels gritty and loose, it's sandy soil. Sandy soils are usually well drained and well aerated. (Having air in the soil is important because roots, earthworms, and other soil organisms need air to survive.)

If your soil feels smooth and greasy, it contains lots of clay. You may already know the drawbacks of clay soil. It stays cold and wet in the spring, delaying planting time for perennials. It's also dense and poorly aerated, so plants may grow more slowly.

If your soil crumbles easily between your fingers and is neither gritty nor smooth, it contains moderate amounts of both sand

Sandy soil

Loamy soil

Clay soil

and clay. This type of soil is called loam. Loam is well aerated and holds moisture well. If you have loam soil, count yourself lucky – your perennials will thrive in it.

You can also grow perennials successfully in sandy or clay soils, as long as you improve them before you plant.

Checking Drainage

Soil drainage is the capacity for water to move through the soil. You can't grow easy-care perennials in soggy soil – their roots don't like such wet conditions. Try a simple test to check how well your soil drains. First, remove the top and bottom from a 1½-litre plastic bottle. Dig a shallow, firm-bottomed hole in the soil where you plan to plant your garden. Slip the bottle into the hole, and fill the bottle with water.

After an hour goes by, check the water level in the bottle. If it has dropped 5 to 10cm, your soil drainage is fine. But if it has dropped less than 5cm, you need to improve the drainage. (See "Four Fixes for Poorly Drained Soil" on page 61.) Soil that drains faster than 10cm per hour may be too dry for many perennials. Adding organic matter such as compost, rotted manure or leafmould will help the soil retain water longer. (See "Recipes for Soil Improvement" on page 64.)

Checking Soil pH

Soil pH is a measure of the acidity or alkalinity of the soil. It's expressed as a number from 0 to 14 (0 is very acid; 14 is very alkaline). The magic numbers for growing most perennials are from 6.0 up to 7.0 (slightly acid to neutral). Some woodland perennials prefer a more acid soil, about 5.5 to 6.5.

It is worth remembering that many acid-loving plants will thrive in neutral soils. Lime-loving plants are even more tolerant as they may grow in slightly acid soils, sometimes down to a pH of 6.5.

It's always a good idea to check pH before you plant perennials. You can pick up a soil-testing kit at your local garden centre. Just follow the instructions on the pack. Adding organic matter should help to nudge your pH into the ideal range. Organic matter brings acid soil closer to neutral and, if it is lime-free, it does the same for alkaline soils too. If your soil is very acidic or alkaline, you may have to take special steps to change the pH, or check out acid-loving or lime-loving plants.

Testing Your Soil

To start a perennials garden with confidence on a brand-new site, test your soil before you prepare a bed. It is worth getting a detailed soil test and several gardening organizations and societies offer a full testing service. In return for a small fee and a soil sample, they will send you a detailed analysis indicating not only the pH but levels of major nutrients, the level of organic matter, and recommendations for any remedial action.

Matching Perennials to Your Soil

Some perennials need a rich diet, while others prefer lean conditions. For example, many silver-leaved perennials do best in sandy soils, but most woodland flowers need plenty of moisture and nutrients. (For a detailed list, see "Perennial Soil

---

FOUR FIXES FOR POORLY DRAINED SOIL

If your soil needs better drainage, try one of these techniques.

● Add soil to raise the planting beds 20cm above ground level. If your natural soil is dense and heavy, combine generous amounts of compost, rotted manure, or leafmould with the soil you use to build up the beds.

● Be sure rainwater drains away from the house and garden. Wet soil in beds near your house may be due to overflowing gutters or a mains water leak. Clean out clogged gutters and drains, and repair leaky pipes.

● Install a small drainage ditch to channel water to a soakaway or drainage area.

● Eliminate hidden layers of compacted soil that prevent water from soaking deep into the soil. Dig deep to find the compacted soil, then break it up with a shovel or garden fork. Work in compost, rotted manure, or leafmould plus some coarse grit to prevent the soil from hardening up again. (When you refill the area where you dug, be sure to put the good topsoil on the surface.)

Preferences" on page 63.) Only the toughest perennials, such as daylilies, tolerate very heavy clay soils. But if you add organic matter to clay soil and some coarse grit to improve the drainage and aeration, you can produce a wonderful site for many perennials, including Siberian iris hybrids (*Iris sibirica*), Japanese anemone

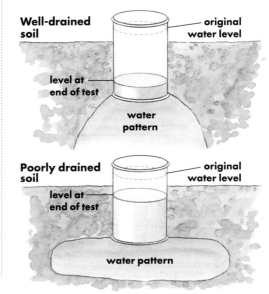

Well-drained soil — original water level

level at end of test

water pattern

Poorly drained soil — original water level

level at end of test

water pattern

◀ **A simple test** using a bottomless bottle shows how well water moves through soil. In well-drained soil, water moves downward easily; in poorly drained soil, it cannot.

▶ **To make growing perennials** even easier, match your plant combinations to your soil conditions. For example, peonies and Siberian irises both thrive in well-drained, moderately fertile soil.

(*Anemone* × *hybrida*), and astilbes.

For an extra-easy perennial garden, choose perennials that grow well in the type of soil you have. When you do, there's little work required to prepare the soil before planting. But if you are desperate to grow your favourite perennials that aren't suited to your soil, you can make raised beds and fill them with a suitable soil mix. Another alternative is to grow them in large tubs.

IMPROVE YOUR SOIL

You can improve any kind of soil by adding

organic matter – compost, rotted manure, composted bark, or leafmould. Straw, grass clippings, and kitchen and garden wastes are best added to the compost heap. Organic matter is the great garden equalizer. It makes lean, dry soils more moist and fertile. It helps open up dense clay soils so that plant roots can penetrate and absorb water and nutrients. Organic matter also releases many nutrients, so it's a really effective natural fertilizer and soil improver.

The best time to improve the soil is in the autumn, before you plant perennials. Once the plants are in place, it's much harder to dig and add amendments.

One precaution: If you plan to turn part of your lawn into a garden, don't just dig or till the grass into the soil below. You'll end up with terrible weed problems. Instead, strip off the turf and compost it grass-side down. Or kill the grass by covering it with a heavy layer of newspaper topped with plastic for up to a year. Once you're sure that all of the weeds and grasses growing in the soil are dead, it's okay to turn under the turf into the soil lying below.

▶ **Autumn is the best time** to add organic matter to your soil. A rotary tiller speeds up the work when you're starting new beds and borders, but make sure the soil is free of perennial weeds first.

PERENNIAL SOIL PREFERENCES

Many perennials can adapt and grow well in less than optimum conditions. But for the healthiest plants, choose perennials that are suited to your soil and site conditions. Here's a rundown of the soil preferences of the easy-care perennials featured in Part 3 of this book.

Light, Lean, Sandy Soil

Artemisia

Coreopsis

Lavandula angustifolia (Lavender)

Salvia officinalis (Garden sage)

Yucca filamentosa (Adam's-needle)

Light, Moderately Fertile Soil

Achillea (Yarrows)

Anemone blanda (Windflower)

Crocus (Crocuses)

Muscari (Grape hyacinths)

Narcissus (Daffodils)

Phlox subulata (Moss phlox)

Pulsatilla vulgaris (Pasque flower)

Scilla (Squills)

Verbena

Well-Drained, Moderately Fertile Soil

Ajuga (Bugles)

Allium

Asclepia tuberosa (Butterfly weed)

Aster × frickartii (Frikart's aster)

Baptisia australis

Calamagrostis × acutiflora (Feather reed grass)

Convallaria majalis (Lily-of-the-valley)

Corydalis lutea (Yellow corydalis)

Crambe cordifolia

Echinacea purpurea

Eranthis hyemalis (Winter aconite)

Geranium (Cranesbills, Hardy geraniums)

Iris sibirica (Siberian iris)

Liatris (Gayfeathers)

Miscanthus sinensis

Paeonia (Peonies)

Phlox maculata (Meadow phlox)

Phlox paniculata (Garden phlox)

Platycodon grandiflorus (Balloon flower)

Rudbeckia (Coneflower)

Scabiosa caucasica (Pincushion flower)

Sedum

Stokesia laevis (Strokes' aster)

Tulipa (Tulips)

Moist, Moderately Fertile Soil

Aster (Michaelmas daisies)

Dicentra (Bleeding hearts)

Eupatorium fistulosum (Joe-Pye weed)

Helleborus (Hellebores)

Heuchera (Coral bells)

Mentha (Mints)

Polygonatum (Solomon's seals)

Pulmonaria (Lungworts)

Tiarella (Foamflowers)

Viola (Pansies, Violets)

Moist, Highly Fertile Soil

Alchemilla mollis (Lady's-mantle)

Anemone (Windflowers)

Aruncus dioicus (Goat's beard)

Asarum (Wild gingers)

Astilbe

Athyrium (Lady ferns, painted ferns)

Brunnera macrophylla

Cimicifuga racemosa (Black snakeroot)

Hosta

Osmunda regalis (Royal fern)

Phlox divaricata (Blue phlox)

Phlox stolonifera (Creeping phlox)

Recipes for Soil Improvement

The following recipes will help you to prepare an ideal soil and enable you to keep it in tip-top condition. Before planting, work the amendments into the top 20 to 30cm of the soil as you dig or fork over the ground.

MOIST, RICH SOIL

● For heavy clay soil, add coarse sand or grit plus organic matter – compost, leafmould, well-rotted manure – before planting. Every following year, add more organic matter as a mulch; fork in the organic material if it has a coarse structure.

● Enrich loam with organic matter when you first prepare the bed. Every year thereafter add more organic matter, as a mulch or forked in as a soil amendment.

● Improve light, sandy soils by adding organic matter generously when you first prepare the bed. Add more organic matter every year, either forked in or as a mulch.

LEAN, LIGHT SOIL

● Keep already-light soils productive by adding organic matter before planting and every year thereafter.

● The structure of heavy clay soil can be improved by adding ground minerals in the form of dolomite or gypsum. Test the pH of your soil (see "Checking your soil pH" on pages 61 and 62) before adding dolomite as it contains calcium and will make your soil more alkaline; gypsum does not have this effect. Apply them at the rates recommended on the packages, but not at the same time as you apply organic materials.

● Drainage of clay soils can be improved still further by mulching with gravel or coarse grit.

Making Compost

Compost is a perennial gardener's all-purpose treasure. Compost happens when you pile together vegetable wastes, shredded leaves, kitchen scraps, and manure and let them decompose. It's a simple process. The end result is dark, crumbly organic matter that will improve your soil, make an excellent mulch, and feed your perennials.

COMPOST INGREDIENTS

Be inventive in finding local sources of compost materials. A mix of dry, brown and moist, green materials gives the best results. Good ingredients include old straw, leaves (shredded are best), wood chips, pulled weeds (without seeds), grass clippings, spent vegetable plants (such as lettuce or spinach), manure, and kitchen scraps.

If you need more materials than you can find in your own garden, offer to take extra leaves and grass clippings from neighbours. If you're using large amounts of wood chips, be sure to balance them with some green, nitrogen-rich materials, or decay will be very slow.

There are some materials you *shouldn't* put in your compost pile: weeds that have gone to seed, persistent perennial weeds (such as ground elder, bindweed, dandelion roots), diseased plants, insect-infested plants, cat and dog droppings, meats, and oils.

▼ **A compost heap in the making** shows clear layers of manure, straw, grass clippings, and garden and kitchen waste. This well-balanced mixture of dry and moist materials will make excellent compost.

COOK UP A BATCH OF FAST COMPOST

Garden centres and mail-order garden suppliers sell attractive plastic and wooden bins that keep a compost heap well hidden, so you don't have to worry that your compost will offend your neighbours or detract from the beauty of your perennial gardens. You can also make a compost heap in a simple bin made of strong wire mesh or slatted boards. Follow these easy steps:

1 Gather your dry brown and fresh green materials at your composting site.

2 Spread a 1-metre-square layer of dry materials in your bin.

3 Wedge a heavy cardboard tube (like a mailing tube) into the centre.

4 Pile up more materials around the tube, mixing dry and moist materials as you go. Add a few handfuls of good garden soil into the mix as you go. (The soil contains the microorganisms that power the decay process.)

5 Over the next few weeks, continue adding materials to the pile until it is 1 metre high. Then stop adding to it and remove the tube to channel air deep into the pile.

6 Mix the materials in the pile with a garden fork every three weeks to encourage fast decay. When the compost is brown and crumbly, it's ready to use.

You can also buy a commercial quick composter. These barrels or rotating bins make turning the pile quick and easy. Simply follow the instructions that come with the composter. However, you can only make a small quantity of compost at a time.

SIMMER A BATCH OF LEAFMOULD

Making leafmould is a long-term, low-effort project. Build a simple wire-mesh bin, 1 metre tall, wide, and deep, and fill it with autumn leaves. Then just let it sit – no turning required! After a year or two the pile will decompose, forming leafmould.

MULCH TO PROTECT YOUR SOIL

Mulching is the finishing touch for an easy-care perennial garden. A layer of organic material buffers the soil (and the living organisms in it, including plant roots) from abrupt changes in temperature. As it breaks down, your perennials get a steady supply of nutrients. Organic mulches must always be spread when the soil is thoroughly moist. Mulches reduce evaporation from the soil, so you won't have to water as often. And mulches discourage weed-seed germination if applied thickly enough.

▲ **Mulch your perennials** with bark chips or other organic mulch to protect the soil and discourage weeds.

A MULCH MENU

Choose mulches that are readily available to you and look good with your plants. This table tells you the ideal depth to spread your mulch to keep weeds at bay, but any mulch is better than none.

Mulch	Thickness	Notes
Bark chips	7–10cm	If fresh they rob soil of nitrogen.
Cocoa shells	7–10cm	Improves soil.
Gravel	3–5cm	Free-draining.
Leafmould	7–10cm	Improves soil.
Garden compost	7–10cm	Improves soil; may attract slugs.

BUYING AND PLANTING PERENNIALS

▼ The advantage of buying plants at a nursery is that you can judge the appearance and health of the plants at first hand.

BUYING PLANTS

Whether you stroll through aisles of green plants at a local nursery or garden centre, or page through the tempting descriptions and photos in mail-order catalogues, you're sure to enjoy the beauty and variety of perennials while you shop. But on the practical level, there are two important decisions to make before you buy. How do you want to buy your plants – potted, with roots, or as seeds? And, if purchasing plants, how many should you buy? To answer these questions, you'll need to weigh how much you're willing to spend against your wish to have a colourful, well-filled garden quickly.

Perennials come in a wide range of prices. You may raise your own plants from seed to get more perennials for your money, but they will take time to reach flowering size and will need much more attention than perennials bought as plants. For perennials that grow from bulbs, like daffodils and tulips, the best choice is to buy and plant dormant bulbs. Whatever you choose, treat the plants carefully, and plant them as soon as possible after you buy.

Bareroot and Field-grow Perennials
Few herbaceous plants are sold bareroot

these days, except for wallflowers (*Erysimum*). These are on sale in autumn from markets, garden centres, nurseries, and by mail order. Once you get your bundle of plants home put the roots in a bucket of lukewarm water for an hour to revive them, then wrap them in moist newspaper until you can get them in the ground. Plant them the same day if possible. (This will be easy if you have the bed ready-prepared.) If you can't plant immediately store the roots in a cool place for several days. All of the above applies equally to plants or small divisions of perennials that you collect from friends or neighbours.

Field-grown plants sold by some nurseries and mail-order operators are usually large, but they also cover plants from friends and relatives. Field-grown plants have survived year-round outdoor temperatures which, according to where they have been growing, prove their hardiness.

Mail-order suppliers lift their plants with a soil ball which is wrapped in a similar way to a rootballed tree or shrub. When plants arrive, keep the rootball moist and plant them in their growing positions as soon as possible. If for any reason you cannot do this straight away, plant them in pots.

Potted Perennials

The most usual way of buying perennials is in small pots. Potted perennials offer an easy start for your garden. They come with a full set of active roots and topgrowth, so they withstand transplanting well. Perennials sent mail order in this way are as young plants growing in small plastic modules. At garden centres and nurseries you can buy more mature plants but, of course, the larger the plant the more expensive it will be. You can plant potted perennials through most of the growing season, except during very hot, dry spells, as long as you water them if the soil gets dry. It's best to plant small potted perennials during moist, cool weather in spring or early autumn. Mail-order plants should be planted as soon as possible after they arrive, or repotted into larger sized pots. In cold or exposed areas put new plants in at least six weeks before the onset of winter, so they can establish.

Bulbs

Bulbs are easy to buy in bulk at nurseries and garden centres. If you want specific cultivars, though, you may need to order your bulbs from mail-order suppliers, and put in your order early to avoid disappointment. Be sure to select firm, heavy bulbs. Buy the biggest bulbs you can afford – they will produce the showiest flowers.

How Many Perennials Should You Buy?

The planting plans in Part 1, beginning on page 8, include recommendations of how many plants you'll need to buy to create the gardens shown. If you follow the plans exactly and use the number of plants recommended, your gardens will look full

---

WILD-COLLECTED PLANTS

Be cautious when buying wildflowers, ferns, and species bulbs. Some nurseries harvest these plants from the wild. Collecting wild plants weakens the native populations; species can become endangered because of wild collecting. Also, the plants harvested may not grow well when transplanted, so wild collecting is bad both for gardeners and the environment. Be sure to buy *nursery-propagated* plants; the phrase "nursery-grown" may be used for plants collected from the wild and then grown for a season at the nursery.

and finished in the first or second season.

If you alter a plan, you'll need to figure out for yourself how many plants to buy. You can judge how far apart to space plants by studying the planting plans. But do give perennials enough room to reach their full size without being overcrowded.

For most perennials, there's a range of possible spacings. Here are two examples: You can plant a large, spreading perennial like Joe-Pye weed (*Eupatorium fistulosum*) from 45 to 60cm apart. For a smaller, clumping plant like sea-pink (*Armeria maritima*), 20cm apart is usual.

You may want to space your perennials a little farther apart than shown in the planting plans. This can save you some money, since you won't need to buy as many plants. Your garden may look a little sparse for the first couple of seasons, but you can fill the gaps with annuals raised from seed.

▼ **Fill gaps** in a new perennial planting by adding annuals from seed or bought as bedding plants in the spaces between perennials.

STEP-BY-STEP PLANTING TECHNIQUE
Planting perennials in well-prepared soil is easy. If you haven't prepared your soil yet, refer to "Soil Care for Beautiful Perennial Gardens", beginning on page 60.

Planting Bareroot Perennials and Divisions
Bareroot perennials and divisions look small and forlorn when you first plant them. Don't worry! With proper care, they'll soon send out lush, new growth. Here's how to get them off to a great start:

1 Soak roots in lukewarm water for an hour before planting. Remove damaged roots and lank foliage.  Dig a hole large enough to hold the roots without curling or twisting.

2 Make a cone of soil in the center to support the plant's crown and keep it just  above soil level. Work the roots gently around the cone. For a taproot plant, dig a long, narrow hole, leaving the crown just above soil level.

3 Fill the hole with soil and tamp it down firmly. Then water thoroughly.

Planting Potted Perennials

With potted perennials, you can test your garden design before you plant. Just set each pot on the spot where you plan to plant it. Then step back and see whether the spacing looks even. Make any adjustments you like, then start the planting process.

1 Turn the pot upside down, supporting the base of the plant with one hand. Tap the sides and base to loosen the rootball, then  slip it out gently. Use your finger to separate tangled roots and loosen matted roots. If the tangles or mattings are severe, use an old kitchen fork to loosen them.

 2 Dig a hole deep and wide enough to hold the roots. Set the plant in the hole. The junction of the stem and roots should be level with the soil surface. If it's not, remove the plant and add soil.

3 Set the plant inside the hole, then fill the hole with soil, working soil around the loose roots as you go. Water the plant slowly and thoroughly.

Planting Field-Grown Perennials

The planting technique for field-grown perennials is very similar to that of potted perennials. The main difference is that you should try to avoid disturbing the roots and rootball – just set the plant in a hole of the proper size, fill it in, and water.

Follow-Up Care For Perennials

Spread a layer of organic mulch around your new perennials. Keep the soil moist until the plants begin to grow strongly.

Planting Bulbs

The best time to plant spring-blooming bulbs is in the autumn.

1 Dig a hole four times as deep as the height of the bulbs you're planting. For instance, for a 2-cm-high bulb, dig a hole 8cm deep. Widen the hole so it can accommodate multiple bulbs without them touching. Set the bulbs on a layer of grit if the soil is wet or heavy.

2 Settle the bulb or bulbs into the hole, root end down. Fill the hole with soil. You can make a two-tiered planting by setting in large bulbs, filling the hole partway with soil, settling smaller bulbs in place, and then topping off the hole with more soil.

3 Tamp the soil down firmly with a rake, then cover the area planted in bulbs with a light mulch such as leafmould. Mark the edges of the bulb planting so you don't accidentally dig into it when planting your other perennials in spring.

PERENNIAL
CARE PRIMER

With a great design, good soil, and proper planting, your easy-care perennial garden will grow beautifully without much extra effort from you. But there are times when you'll need to come to the rescue with basic care like watering, fertilizing, and weeding. And there are a few special techniques that you can use to keep your perennial garden beautiful, neat, and healthy, like staking, deadheading, and dividing. Read on for directions on each technique.

WATERING WISDOM

More isn't always better when it comes to watering. Newly planted perennials and moisture-loving perennials may need regular watering until they are established. But many other perennials need no extra water in climates with regular rainfall. And perennials that prefer lean, dry soil may need watering only during droughts. (See "Perennial Soil Preferences" on page 63 to learn more about the moisture needs of specific plants.)

If you do water established perennials, don't just go over them lightly with the hose. Water deeply. A general rule is that plants need 2 to 3cm of water each week, from rainfall or watering. (They'll need even more during very hot, dry weather.) For young plants with small or shallow root systems, water more frequently so that the top layer of soil stays moist.

▼ **Newly planted** or moisture-loving perennials need regular, deep watering. A soaker, or seep, hose snaking between the plants supply them with water.

The easiest and most effective way to water is with trickle or soaker hoses. Because this type of irrigation releases moisture at ground level, it loses little to evaporation. Unlike overhead sprinkling, trickle irrigation won't wet leaves, which can encourage plant diseases and is less wasteful.

You can customize a moderately priced drip or trickle irrigation system for your garden. Run small irrigation tubes to every plant or group of plants, selecting different moisture emitters (devices that release water at a specific rate) to provide more water to thirsty plants and less to plants that prefer drier soil. You can hook the irrigation system up to a timer that will automatically turn the system on and off, even when you aren't home. For details, contact a specialist supplier or mail-order garden supply company that offers drip or trickle irrigation kits.

An inexpensive alternative is soaker hoses. Snake these between plants in a bed. To water, attach your regular garden hose and set it for a slow flow. Soaker hoses have a few disadvantages. Water tends to seep out more quickly at the end closest to the water supply. Also, soaker hoses can clog or kink, cutting off the flow to some parts of the garden.

FERTILIZING FACTS

Like people, some perennials need more food than others. It's as important to avoid overfertilizing as it is underfertilizing. Slow growth, poor flowering, and discoloured foliage are all signs that your perennials are struggling. Overgrown, floppy foliage is a sign that a plant is in soil that's too rich for its needs. Perennials that prefer lean soil are more prone to disease when they grow in rich soil. This shows how important it is to match your perennials to your soil type. For guidelines on the soil preferences of the perennials in Part 3 of this book, see "Perennial Soil Preferences" on page 63.

Heavy-feeding perennials, especially mature plants, benefit from regular feeding. Many other perennials grow beautifully without extra nutrients if they're planted in fertile soil and mulched with compost. But in lean soil, be sure to fertilize in spring and again before flowering. For more details on when to fertilize perennials, see "Easy-Care Fertilizing" on page 72.

Using Organic Fertilizers

Use a balanced organic fertilizer for perennials, one with a modest percentage of nitrogen and ample amounts of phosphorus and potassium. You can find organic fertilizer blends at most garden

▼ **No extra feeding** is required for many easy-care perennials, including rudbeckias, verbenas, and crocosmias. Just plant them in fertile soil and mulch with compost.

centres; read the label to make sure the product contains only natural ingredients like composted bark, composted manure, hoof and horn, blood meal, bonemeal, fish meal, rock potash, rock phosphate, or seaweed extracts.

Look for a packaged organic fertilizer labelled 2-4-4 or 4-6-6 (these numbers indicate the percentages of nitrogen, phosphorus, and potassium, respectively, in the product). A balanced fertilizer encourages strong root and flower formation as well as steady growth. Apply fertilizer blends according to the instructions on the package.

Liquid fertilizers such as fish emulsion, liquid comfrey, and seaweed extract will give your plants a quick boost in growth, but they won't have a long-lasting effect. To brew your own liquid feed, put a shovelful of compost in a sack, and soak it in a 20 litre plastic container full of water for two or three days. Remove the bag (you can put the compost back in your compost pile), and dilute the liquid until it is the colour of weak tea, and use it to fertilize your garden.

Slow-release fertilizers, such as bone meal and hoof and horn, release nutrients gradually over a period of weeks or months. Rock potash (a good source of potassium) can work for several years, offering a remedy for a potassium deficiency.

▲ **Remove large weeds** by pulling firmly at the base of the stem. If the weeds don't yield, loosen the roots with a hand fork and pull again.

WIPING OUT WEEDS

Weeding makes your gardens look neat, but more important, it eliminates hiding places for pests and diseases to build up and prevents unwanted plants from crowding out your flowers. Take special care to control weeds in a newly planted bed. Weed seeds sprout easily in the newly worked soil and in the open spaces between young perennial plants. When you first prepare a bed, be sure to remove all of the perennial weed roots you find. Try these strategies for controlling weeds:

● Prevent lawngrass from creeping into perennial beds by installing a brick edging between the bed and the lawn.

EASY-CARE FERTILIZING

Plan your fertilizing schedule according to the natural needs of your plants.

For perennials that prefer rich soil: When the first shoots emerge in spring, pull back the mulch around the plants, and sprinkle a balanced granular organic blended fertilizer around the edges of the shoots. Use a trowel or hand fork to work it lightly into the soil. Then, if the soil is moist, add a fresh mulch of finished compost. If growth seems weak in early summer or before bloom, give a liquid feed.

For perennials that thrive in lean soil: Add a light mulch of finished compost around the edges of emerging plants in spring when the soil is moist. If growth is still slow in early summer, try giving the plants a liquid feed.

For spring-flowering bulbs: Side dress with a balanced organic fertilizer blend in early autumn. In summer, allow the bulb foliage to yellow before removing it.

▲ **To keep tough weeds down,** cover the soil with several layers of newspaper topped with organic mulch.

● After planting, cover open areas with several layers of newspaper topped with an organic mulch. You can substitute black polythene or landscape fabric for the newspaper.

● In places where you cannot mulch, run a hoe over the soil surface at least once a week during spring and early summer to uproot any weed seedlings that appear. Hand-pull large weeds, tugging gently at the base of the stems or using a hand fork to uproot them.

● If a weed is growing snugly against a perennial, cut off the intruder with secateurs to avoid damaging the perennial.

● For seedy weeds, put a plastic bread bag over your hand and arm, grab the weed, pull the plastic down over the weed, and bag it up. You can throw away the seedy weeds and reuse the bag. For spiny or rash-inducing weeds wear gardening gloves and long sleeves.

STAKING STRATEGIES

Perennials with narrow stems or full, heavy flowers are prone to flopping. Delicate stems may simply bend, but stronger stems may break at the base. Most of the easy-care perennials in this book are self-supporting. The exceptions are tall Michaelmas daisies and rudbeckias. (Some gardeners like the cascading look of these plants when left to flop, while others want the upright impact of staked plants.) Other perennials will

▼ **Use plant stakes** to keep your perennials from falling flat. Linking plant stakes (*below left*) work well for groups of upright perennials. Hoop supports (*below*) are a good choice for floppy perennials.

▶ **Deadheading** with hedge clippers can save time for large clumps of perennials like lady's-mantle or bee balm (bergamot) that hold their flowers above the foliage.

occasionally need staking if they develop lush growth due to too rich or warm wet conditions, or if you accidentally site sun-lovers in partial shade.

There are several ways to support floppy perennials. The key is to put the support in place long before a plant falls flat on its face in your garden.

● Let perennials lean on sturdy neighbours such as a shrub, bearded iris, or hosta.

● Pinch back low- to moderate-size bushy perennials, such as coreopsis and 'Autumn Joy' sedum, in midspring. They will branch out, stay compact, and be less likely to flop.

● Set a low, wire-mesh cage over an emerging bushy plant. The stems will grow through the cage. Once the stems fill out, they will hide the wire.

● Train plants that need support at the base through wire hoops or squares of linking stakes.

● Tie perennials with upright flower spikes to individual bamboo stakes that are almost as tall as the mature flower stem. Put the stakes in place in spring. As the flower stems grow, gently tie them to the stakes with strips of tights or with soft, green plant ties.

DEADHEADING DETAILS

If you let your perennials set seed, they'll use lots of their energy producing the seed instead of more leaves and flowers. Also, the seeds may scatter around the garden, resulting in hundreds of seedlings that can be as pesky as weeds. To prevent both of these problems, deadhead – remove flowers as they fade, before they set seed.

Deadheading prolongs flowering of many easy-care perennials, including yarrows (*Achillea*), lady's-mantle (*Alchemilla mollis*), thrift (*Armeria maritima*), coreopsis, bleeding hearts (*Dicentra*), *Echinacea purpurea*, daylily (*Hemerocallis*), *Phlox maculata*, salvias, pincushion flower (*Scabiosa caucasica*), and Stokes' aster (*Stokesia laevis*). When you deadhead, you can cut off the old flowers one by one or remove entire flowering stems after all of the flower buds have opened. But look closely before you cut because some unopened flower buds may be hidden below the faded flowers. If you find some, just snip off the faded blooms above, so you can enjoy the flowers beneath.

Some perennials have such attractive seedheads that you won't want to deadhead them. These include butterfly weed (*Asclepias tuberosa*), astilbes, blue false indigo (*Baptisia australis*), *Echinacea purpurea*, *Rudbeckia fulgida*, Lenten rose (*Helleborus orientalis*), and many ornamental grasses, which continue to look good through the winter months.

DIVIDENDS OF DIVIDING

Over the years, many perennials creep outward, overgrowing neighbouring plants. Some perennials become hollow in the centre as they spread. Bulbs may stop flowering with age. The easy cure to all of these problems is division – the simple process of lifting a plant and cutting or pulling sections of the roots apart.

Replanting the sections in fresh soil rejuvenates the plant as well as the garden.

Bulbs are especially easy to divide. As the foliage yellows, unearth the bulbs and separate the mature mother bulbs from the smaller offspring. Enrich the soil with compost, and replant with the flat end where the roots will grow on the bottom and the pointed shoot end facing up.

You can divide a large perennial clump into three moderate-size clumps that you can replant to create a lovely grouping. Or replant just the young outer portions and discard the rest. If you're expanding your gardens and want lots of new plants to fill them, you can divide the clump into a dozen small sections, each with at least a couple of shoots and roots.

Divide summer- or autumn-blooming perennials in spring, as the shoots emerge from the ground. Divide spring-blooming perennials in late summer or early autumn. Perennials with many fibrous roots, such as Japanese anemones (*Anemone × hybrida*) and bugles (*Ajuga*), are easy to break apart with your hands.

For fleshy-rooted perennials such as daylilies (*Hemerocallis*), dig up the clump, use a hose to wash off the soil, then roll the plant on the ground to loosen the roots. Divide by hand or prise apart with two garden forks inserted back to back into the clump. You may have to use a knife or spade to cut through the roots of older plants.

Not all perennials need dividing. Some, including butterfly weed (*Asclepias tuberosa*) and blue false indigo (*Baptisia australis*), have long taproots that can't be cut apart. Other perennials, such as astilbes, hostas, Siberian iris, and peonies, grow slowly into magnificent mature plants that seldom need to be rejuvenated.

HEADING OFF PROBLEMS

When you keep up with seasonal chores like watering, fertilizing, and deadheading, your perennials usually grow and bloom without problems. In general, the easy-care perennials recommended in this book aren't prone to pest or disease problems. But if you find signs of insects or disease, look for the solutions in the "Perennial Problem Solver", beginning on page 76, and take prompt action to keep the trouble from spreading any further.

▲ **To divide tough clumps** of perennials or ferns, insert two garden forks back to back, and then push the handles apart.

PERENNIAL PROBLEM SOLVER

The easy-care perennials recommended in this book are generally trouble-free. But occasionally they may need a little attention to prevent or control problems.

PREVENTING DISEASE PROBLEMS

If you've planted your perennials in the right soil and sun or shade conditions, you're off to a good start in preventing disease problems. Choosing disease-resistant or disease-tolerant types and cultivars also helps you sidestep some common diseases of perennials. Most disease organisms need moist conditions to thrive, so good air circulation around your plants will help lower humidity.

Despite these precautions, you may find plants in your garden that have blemished or rotted leaves, stems, or roots. When you do, always remove the diseased plant parts, and burn them or dispose of them. This helps to prevent the problem from spreading.

PREVENTING AND CONTROLLING PESTS

To control pests (and also diseases), you have to know what you're dealing with. Inspect the plant to find the culprit or samples of the damage it causes. "Solving Problems", opposite, will help you decide what kind of pest is feasting on your plant. Once you've identified the pest, find out how you can eliminate its hiding places or overwintering haunts. Good garden cleanup practices, like removing and composting old leaves and stems, may be all it takes. Also, choose a control method that does the least damage to the garden environment. Barriers and traps are a great way to start. Barriers range from a high fence to keep out deer, to a gravel mulch to deter slugs. Slugs can also be drowned in a simple beer trap (see opposite). If you have to use a spray, use a mild, organic product labelled for that particular pest. Read the label and follow directions carefully to be sure the results will be safe and effective.

BENEFICIAL INSECTS AND PARASITES

When you garden organically you'll attract powerful problem preventers – beneficial insects. Ladybirds, lacewings, spiders, and other insect predators eat plant-eating pests and act as a natural biological control. Tiny wasps and other beneficial parasites lay their eggs in the bodies of pest insects. After they hatch the larvae eat the pests from the inside. Populations of beneficials will increase when you plant a variety of flowers for alternative food sources. Most important, to encourage beneficials, don't use insecticides.

You can buy some types of biological control from garden centres or by mail order, and release them in your garden. Follow the instructions on the package carefully when applying biological controls.

USE SOAPS AND SPRAYS

Spraying your perennials with insecticidal soap will kill soft-bodied insects. Soaps are nontoxic to animals and most beneficial insects but control aphids, whiteflies, leafhoppers, red spider mites, and other pests. Spray according to the product instructions.

SOLVING PROBLEMS

Check this chart to identify and control the most common pest and disease problems in the perennial garden.

PESTS

Symptom	Pest Description	Pest Name	Control
Leaves with large, ragged holes; slime trails on leaves	Soft-bodied grey, black, or brown creatures with or without a hard shell	Slug or snail	Set out beer traps (a saucer of beer set at soil level), mulch plants with gravel or sharp sand.
Distorted shoots and leaves; sticky, sometimes black-coated stems and leaves	Tiny, soft-bodied, pear-shaped insects	Aphids	Encourage beneficial insects; spray with insecticidal soap.
Brown tunnels in leaves	Pale green maggots, not visible on outside of leaf	Leafminers	Remove and destroy infested leaves.
Discoloured, speckled leaves in hot dry summers	Specks or webbing on underside of leaves	Red spider mites	Keep plants well watered; spray with water.

Slug

Aphids

Leafminer damage

DISEASES

Symptom	Disease	Control
Blackened, curling flowers on peony buds; brown leaf spots	Botrytis (grey mould)	Remove and destroy infected plants; thin plants to improve air circulation.
Rusty spots on underside of leaves	Rust	Remove and destroy infected plants; apply sulphur dust to prevent spread.
White coating on new leaves during hot and dry, or humid weather	Mildew	Plant resistant cultivars; apply a baking soda spray; if problems have been severe in the past, apply sulphur spray.
Wilting leaves and stems; rotten roots or crown	Root and crown rots	Remove and destroy infected plant parts; replant in soil with better drainage.

Easy-Care Perennial Encyclopedia

Once you've decided which of the easy-care gardens from "Easy-Care Garden Designs" you want to plant, and boned up on the perennial gardening techniques covered in "Easy-Care Basics," you'll want more details on the specific perennials you plan to try. The following rundown of 60 easy-care perennials will supply all the information you need to grow and use these terrific plants in your garden.

Plant Names

To find plants in this "Easy-Care Perennial Encyclopedia", look for them alphabetically by botanical name. Botanical names include genus and species names. For example, the botanical name for common peony is *Paeonia officinalis*. It's a good idea to become familiar with botanical names of perennials, because they're listed that way in garden centres and catalogues. Of course, each entry also lists the most familiar common names for each perennial. So if you don't know the botanical name of a particular plant, look up its common name in the index to find the page listing for the plant.

Appearance

Each plant entry includes descriptions of the perennial, including the best cultivars. Cultivars are special variations developed by plant breeders; a cultivar has particular characteristics like flower colour, size, and disease resistance that make it desirable. You'll find all the cultivars used in the garden designs in "Easy-Care Garden Designs", and more besides.

Garden Uses

In this section of each entry, I've suggested groups of perennials that look good and grow well together, so you can dabble in creating your own designs.

Growing and Propagation

In this section, you'll find tips on planting and caring for each perennial that will help you keep it in top form. I've also given instructions on when and how to propagate to increase your supply of plants.

Baptisia australis
BLUE FALSE INDIGO

Add height and interesting texture to perennial beds with the cloverlike leaves and striking blue flowers of blue false indigo.

Blue false indigo flowers add valuable early-summer colour to a bed or border, but the blue green foliage is an asset too.

APPEARANCE Blue false indigo has spikes of bright blue flowers that rise from 60 to 120cm tall. The blue-green leaves, which resemble clover, were once fermented to produce a blue dye. The dark seedpods remain interesting long after the flowers have faded.

GARDEN USES Use blue false indigo in the middle or rear of a flower garden. The cool blue flowers are a perfect complement to pink peonies, bleeding hearts (*Dicentra*), and cranesbills (*Geranium*). They contrast nicely with silver artemisia foliage or with golden and orange flowers, such as fern-leaved *Achillea millefolium*.

GROWING AND PROPAGATION Plant in full sun and fertile, well-drained soil. In open or lightly shaded sites, let the plant grow up through a supporting ring or grid. Deadhead to encourage a long period of bloom or allow the seedpods to form for summer and autumn interest. This is one perennial that stays put in the garden and won't require division. To increase your supply of plants, take cuttings from the tips of stems after flowering ends.

Plant Profile

HARDINESS
Hardy

SEASON OF BLOOM
Late spring and early summer

LIGHT REQUIREMENTS

MOISTURE REQUIREMENTS

HEIGHT
60 to 120cm

SPREAD
75 to 100cm

How to Use the Plant Profiles

For quick details such as season of bloom, moisture requirements, and height,
check the "Plant Profile" feature in each plant entry. Here's what you'll find.

1 Hardiness

Hardiness refers to whether a perennial can tolerate frost. However, other factors influence perennial survival over winter, such as maturity, plant health, and moisture levels, both in the soil and in the air. For example, some plants which can tolerate sub-zero temperatures for long periods providing the air is dry, succumb in a dank moist, albeit frost-free environment. A winter mulch is applied not just to protect plant roots from cold, but also from excessive moisture.

Consider hardiness as a guideline, rather than a hard-and-fast rule. You may want to experiment with a less-than-hardy plant by planting it in well-drained soil and a warm location near your house or a sheltering wall. But for a truly easy-care perennials garden it's wise to stick with plants that are reliably hardy in your local area. That means selecting species that are completely hardy and won't need special care to thrive.

For the purposes of this book plant hardiness is defined as follows. Hardy plants are able to survive winter outdoors, while plants of borderline hardiness, or frost tender, may come through unscathed but, unless planted in an area with reliably mild winters or in a sheltered position, benefit from winter protection.

2 Season of Bloom

This covers the range of times when species of a given perennial may be in bloom. For example, the phlox entry lists bloom times of spring and summer. This reflects the fact that there are spring-flowering phloxes like creeping phlox, and summer bloomers like garden phlox. Check the descriptions in the entry for details on when a particular species of perennial blooms.

3 Light Requirements

Sunlight is another critical factor that influences how well perennials perform. Some perennials require full sun – about 6 hours or more of direct sunlight each day. In

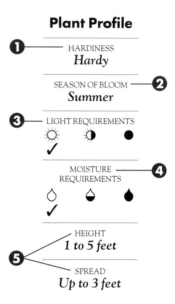

Plant Profile

① ——— HARDINESS
Hardy

SEASON OF BLOOM ——— ②
Summer

③ ——— LIGHT REQUIREMENTS

MOISTURE ——— ④
REQUIREMENTS

⑤ ——— HEIGHT
1 to 5 feet

SPREAD
Up to 3 feet

the Plant Profiles, these perennials have a tick below the unshaded sun symbol. If your border is in light shade and only receives 4 to 6 hours of sun a day, it's best not to attempt to grow sun-loving perennials. You'll have plenty of great choices among perennials that thrive in partial shade (indicated by a tick below the half-darkened sun). For plants that do well in full shade or less than 4 hours of sun a day, look for a tick below the fully darkened sun.

full sun   partial shade   full shade

4 Moisture Requirements

The water droplet symbol in the Plant Profiles indicates moisture requirements. Moisture levels tend to be higher in clay soil and soils rich in organic matter; they're also higher in climates with abundant rainfall. Drier soils tend to occur in sandy areas or where rainfall is light. Plants such as lavender that require soil that is on the dry side have a tick below the unfilled water droplet. For evenly moist, well-drained soil, look for perennials marked with a tick below the half-filled droplet. Plants that need constantly moist soils are noted by a tick below the filled-in droplet.

low moisture   moderate   high moisture
                     moisture

5 Height and Spread

Use the height and spread information in the Plant Profiles to help you plan your own garden. Set tall plants back far enough in the garden so they won't block your view of shorter plants. When you plant new gardens, or slip a perennial into an opening in an existing garden, give the plants enough room to fill out to their mature spread. This prevents overcrowding and helps keep perennials healthy.

Armed with all this great information, you'll be well prepared for planting and enjoying your easy-care perennial garden. You'll be rewarded for your efforts with a garden full of beautiful flowers for years to come.

Achillea
YARROW

*Add a feathery touch to a sunny garden with
yarrow's ferny foliage and abundant,
long-lasting flowers.*

'Coronation Gold' yarrow adds vibrant yellow flowers to a mixed border throughout the summer.

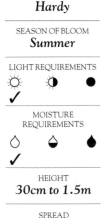

grows to 1 metre tall, has grey-tinted foliage, and produces golden flowers for up to 3 months. It grows well in humid summers.

Common yarrow (*A. millefolium*) has handsome pink, red, or white flowers on branching stems that may need staking for support. Cultivars include orangy-red 'Paprika' and pastel pink 'Apple Blossom'. Woolly yarrow (*A. tomentosa*) forms a mat of furry grey foliage with golden flowers on stems to 25cm tall.

GARDEN USES Use woolly yarrow to edge an herb or perennial garden. Taller yarrows are great for the middle or rear of a flower border or island bed. Try combining 'Coronation Gold' with *Salvia* × *superba* and *Miscanthus sinensis* var. *strictus*.

GROWING AND PROPAGATION Plant yarrow in full sun and light, well-drained soil of moderate fertility. The stems may need support to stay upright. Once established, yarrow is drought-tolerant. Avoid fertilizing except in very poor soils. Divide every three years, or as needed to encourage blooming and prevent excessive spread. Remove faded flowers, cutting back to new flower buds. Remove spent flower stems at their base to keep the plant tidy and prevent self-sowing.

APPEARANCE Yarrows have finely cut leaves that spread in feathery mats near the ground. Most have large flat-topped clusters of small yellow, white, pink, or red flowers.

'Moonshine', a hybrid yarrow, grows up to 60cm tall with soft yellow flowers and grey-tinted foliage. It does best in warm, dry summers, in a sunny situation.

Fernleaved *A. filipendulina* is a bold, golden-flowered yarrow that reaches 1 to 1.5 metres tall. The more compact cultivar 'Cloth of Gold' grows 60cm to 1.2 metres.

The hybrid A. 'Coronation Gold'

Plant Profile

HARDINESS
Hardy

SEASON OF BLOOM
Summer

LIGHT REQUIREMENTS
☼ ◐ ●
✓

MOISTURE REQUIREMENTS
◊ ◖ ◆
✓

HEIGHT
30cm to 1.5m

SPREAD
Up to 60cm

Ajuga
BUGLE, AJUGA

*Carpet a bed or shady corner with bugle's
clear blue flower spikes and neat
ground-hugging foliage.*

APPEARANCE Bugles are creeping groundcovers that grow into mats of handsome rounded leaves punctuated in spring by abundant spikes of small tubular blossoms.

Blue-flowered *A. genevensis* reaches 15 to 30cm tall in bloom; it may also have pink or white flowers.

Upright bugle *A. pyramidalis* stays lower, about 23cm tall when covered with blue flower spikes. The cultivar 'Metallica Crispa' has wavy, crinkled purple leaves that get darker in the autumn.

Common bugle (*A. reptans*) is 25cm tall when in bloom, with flowers of a beautiful clear blue. Several cultivars are more ornamental: 'Atropurpurea' has purple leaves; 'Burgundy Glow' foliage is a rainbow of white, pink, and green; and 'Multicolor' has bronze leaves marked with purplish pink and cream, and looks even better when the flowers are removed.

GARDEN USES Let bugle spread across the foreground of an island bed or form a carpet to edge a flower or shrub border. 'Burgundy Glow' looks great in light shade combined with pink astilbes and white-edged hostas. Common bugle will spread eagerly into and sometimes over neighbouring plants; use a barrier to keep it in place or give it space so you can enjoy its cheerful spring display.

GROWING AND PROPAGATION
Bugles are carefree, adaptable plants that grow well in sun or shade. They'll spread at a moderate rate in average soil; in rich, loose, moist soil, they'll cover ground rapidly. Remove faded flower spikes to keep the plants tidy. Divide as needed to control size and increase your bugle collection. If sections die back, dig them out and throw away the dead plants. Refill the area with fresh soil and replant new starts of bugle.

For a stylish groundcover, try *Ajuga reptans* 'Catlin's Giant', which develops large leaves and showy blue flower spikes.

Plant Profile

HARDINESS
Hardy

SEASON OF BLOOM
Late spring and early summer

LIGHT REQUIREMENTS
☼ ◐ ●
✓ ✓ ✓

MOISTURE REQUIREMENTS
◊ ◒ ●
✓ ✓

HEIGHT
15 to 30cm

SPREAD
30cm to a metre or more

Alchemilla mollis
LADY'S-MANTLE

Give lady's-mantle a place of honour in the front of the border where its dew-spangled foliage and clouds of airy chartreuse blossoms can be admired.

Lady's-mantle forms rounded mounds of foliage topped by yellow-green flowers that make an attractive groundcover.

Plant Profile

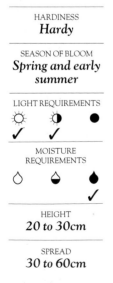

HARDINESS
Hardy

SEASON OF BLOOM
Spring and early summer

LIGHT REQUIREMENTS

MOISTURE REQUIREMENTS

HEIGHT
20 to 30cm

SPREAD
30 to 60cm

APPEARANCE Short, frothy sprays of chartreuse flowers emerge from a clump of attractive round, pleated leaves. The leaves are lightly covered with hairs that catch morning dew or raindrops and sparkle in the sunlight. The plant forms a neat mound to 30cm tall.

GARDEN USES The long-lasting flowers and handsome leaves of lady's-mantle are lovely companions for many perennials. Plant groups of three or five in the front or middle of a perennial border. The unusual colour of the flowers looks surprisingly pretty paired with blues, purples, and yellows. Try planting lady's-mantle with yellow irises and orange butterfly weed (*Asclepias tuberosa*). It also makes a beautiful edging plant or groundcover for a flower or shrub border.

GROWING AND PROPAGATION
Lady's-mantle needs moist, rich soil. It is reasonably drought tolerant, but if conditions become too dry, the leaf margins will turn brown. Plant in full sun or light shade. To rejuvenate foliage, cut it back in midsummer and let the leaves resprout. Divide clumps as needed, although it will self-seed freely. Remove faded flower stems to keep the plant neat and encourage extended bloom.

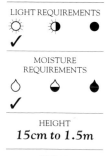

Allium
ALLIUM,
ORNAMENTAL ONIONS

*Add a spark to your perennial garden with the spiky pink flower globes
or white starry flower clusters of these delightful onion relatives.*

APPEARANCE These ornamental members of the onion family have globe-shaped clusters of small white, pink, purple, or yellow flowers. The leaves often carry a hint of onion odour; some have flowers which are sweet smelling. Alliums grow from bulbs that produce slim, linear leaves.

Giant *A. giganteum* sends up large, purple flowerheads on bare stems to 1.5 metres tall.

A. senescens has twisting, 30-cm green or grey leaves that persist through the summer. It bears reddish purple flower clusters up to 60cm tall. The variety *glaucum* has handsome silver leaves to 15cm tall and pink flowers to 40cm tall in late summer and autumn.

Common chives (*A. schoeno-prasum*) grows in a neat tuft of upright foliage that lasts all season and has pink to purple flowers to 45cm tall.

Garlic chives (*A. tuberosum*) has flat, straplike dark green leaves that reach 40cm long and last all season. The foliage has a mild garlic scent and flavour, while the white flowers, borne in late summer and autumn, smell like roses.

GARDEN USES Use tall alliums with leaves that remain all summer, such as chives, in the middle of a perennial garden. The silver foliage of *A. senescens* var. *glaucum* makes an interesting garden edging. Plant

A. *giganteum* and other tall, bare-stemmed alliums between clumps of leafy perennials such as cranesbills (*Geranium*) and lady's-mantle (*Alchemilla mollis*). For a beautiful and aromatic combination, grow chives with lavender and garden sage (*Salvia officinalis*).

GROWING AND PROPAGATION Alliums grow well in full sun with fertile, well-drained soil. To increase your plants, divide the bulbs or rhizomes as the foliage begins to die back. Some alliums, including chives, will self-sow freely. Making divisions is easier than trans-planting seedlings, so deadhead promptly to avoid having to weed out seedlings.

Rounded *Allium senescens* flowers add a splash of late-summer colour. Deadhead the plants promptly to prevent self-seeding.

Plant Profile

HARDINESS
Borderline to fully hardy

SEASON OF BLOOM
Spring, summer, and autumn

LIGHT REQUIREMENTS
☀ ◑ ●
✓

MOISTURE REQUIREMENTS
◇ ◐ ◆
✓

HEIGHT
15cm to 1.5m

SPREAD
10 to 60cm

Anemone
ANEMONE, WINDFLOWER

*Charming anemone blossoms will add grace to
a woodland wildflower garden or a mixed border
in shade or sun.*

White Japanese anemones like 'Honorine Jobert' are a great choice for mixed borders with rich, well-drained soil.

Plant Profile

HARDINESS
Hardy

SEASON OF BLOOM
Spring, summer, or autumn

LIGHT REQUIREMENTS
☀ ☽ ●
✓ ✓

MOISTURE REQUIREMENTS
◦ ◖ ●
✓ ✓

HEIGHT
15cm to 1.5m

SPREAD
20 to 60cm

APPEARANCE Anemones have round, open flowers with clusters of golden stamens in the centre. Some species are low-growing; others send up tall flowerstalks. The leaves usually are deeply lobed.

Snowdrop anemone (A. *sylvestris*) has white flowers to 45cm tall in spring and sometimes in autumn. The fluffy seedheads can be ornamental too.

Japanese anemone (A. × *hybrida*) blooms in late summer or autumn. It grows 1 to 1.5 metres tall with pink or white flowers to 10cm across. Good cultivars include white 'Honorine Jobert'; double-flowered white 'Whirlwind'; compact, double-flowered pink 'Prinz Heinrich';

and pink 'Königin Charlotte'.

The windflower (A. *blanda*) produces blue, pink, or white flowers to 20cm tall in spring, then becomes dormant.

A close relative of the anemones is the pasque flower (*Pulsatilla vulgaris*), another spring bloomer. It grows to 25cm tall with white or purple flowers. It also produces attractive furry buds and leaves and feathery seedheads.

GARDEN USES Scatter tubers of A. *blanda* and its cultivars in groups through any bed for spring colour. Use snowdrop anemones and pasque flowers in the front or middle of a flower border, or let them spread in a woodland garden. Combine them with bloodroot (*Sanguinaria canadensis*) and variegated Solomon's seal (*Polygonatum odoratum* 'Variegatum'). Japanese anemones are nice for the rear of a border. Or put them in masses of five or seven between shrubs.

GROWING AND PROPAGATION Plant Japanese and snowdrop anemones in rich, moist but well-drained soil in sun to light shade. Pasque flowers and *Anemone blanda* form tubers; they need fast-draining soil in light shade or sun. Divide snowdrop and Japanese anemones as needed to control their spread.

Armeria maritima
SEA-PINK, THRIFT

The tidy cushions of thrift accented by pink flowers lend a formal touch to the edge of a sunny perennial bed.

Laucheana thrift makes a showy display of bright pink ball-shaped flowers and grassy foliage.

APPEARANCE Armerias bear neat mounds of evergreen, grasslike foliage. Elegant round clusters of pink or white flowers rise on slim stems to 20cm tall in late spring and reappear sporadically through the summer if deadheaded regularly. Cultivars offer a variety of colours including white 'Alba', dark pink 'Vindictive', and red 'Düsseldorf Pride'. 'Laucheana' has pink flowers and tufty grasslike foliage. A. 'Bees' Ruby' grows to 30cm tall with red flowers and slightly broader leaves than A. *maritima*.

GARDEN USES Use thrift to edge a flower or shrub border; the foliage will stay neat and green year-round and the flowers are attractive for an extended period.

You can also use thrift in rock gardens, gravel gardens, or in sunny crevices, where it flourishes due to the excellent drainage. Thrift is a natural for seaside gardens; it tolerates salty soil and sea spray. It combines well with blue false indigo (*Baptisia australis*) and white peonies.

GROWING AND PROPAGATION Plant in full sun and well-drained sandy or loamy soil. Avoid fertilizing, which can cause the foliage to flop open in the centre. Once growing vigorously, this plant copes well with drought. Remove faded flowers regularly to extend period of bloom. Divide plants in the autumn to renew them or to increase your supply of thrift.

Plant Profile

HARDINESS
Hardy

SEASON OF BLOOM
Late spring and summer

LIGHT REQUIREMENTS
☼ ◑ ●
✓

MOISTURE REQUIREMENTS
◌ ◓ ●
✓ ✓

HEIGHT
15 to 30cm

SPREAD
20 to 30cm

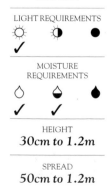

Artemisia
ARTEMISIA, WORMWOOD

Highlight your perennial garden all season long with the aromatic silver foliage of artemisia.

The graceful silver foliage of 'Powis Castle' artemisia can become leggy. To prevent this, cut back old or winter-damaged plants in late spring.

A. *schmidtiana* grows into a low mound to 60cm tall.

GARDEN USES Use low-growing artemisias such as A. *schmidtiana* to edge a flower border or herb garden, or in front of shrubs. They look great with lavender and pink-flowered yarrows (*Achillea*). Use taller artemisias such as 'Powis Castle' to provide contrast with the green foliage of rudbeckias or bronze foliage of 'Palace Purple' heuchera (*Heuchera* 'Palace Purple'). A. *ludoviciana* 'Silver Queen' makes a bold groundcover for sunny areas.

Plant Profile

HARDINESS
Borderline to fully hardy

SEASON OF BLOOM
Summer and autumn

LIGHT REQUIREMENTS
☀ ◑ ●
✓

MOISTURE REQUIREMENTS
◊ ◖ ◕
✓ ✓

HEIGHT
30cm to 1.2m

SPREAD
50cm to 1.2m

APPEARANCE Artemisia's most striking feature is its silver foliage, which adds sparkle to any garden. One of the best is 'Powis Castle', which can grow 75cm tall and 1 metre wide, bearing finely cut silvery white foliage.

'Silver Queen' is a splendid cultivar of A. *ludoviciana* that reaches 75cm tall and a spread of 75cm or more.

GROWING AND PROPAGATION Plant in full sun and average, well-drained soil. Avoid fertilizing. Divide artemisias as needed to control size and keep growth compact and upright. Propagate shrubby 'Powis Castle' by taking stem cuttings rather than dividing. Cut back as needed to keep the plants neat.

Aruncus dioicus
GOAT'S BEARD

Give a lightly shaded garden an elegant centrepiece with the feathery, creamy white spires of this stately perennial.

Goat's beard plants come in male and female forms. Male plants like these produce showier flower plumes, but flowers on female plants turn into lovely ornamental seedheads.

APPEARANCE Feathery white flower plumes rise over fernlike foliage. Each leaf has many broad, oval leaflets; leaves extend up to 1 metre long. Goat's beard may grow only to 1 metre, but can reach as tall as 2 metres. One reliably compact cultivar is 'Kneiffii', which grows to 1 metre tall.

GARDEN USES Goat's beard provides impressive foliage and big, bold flower sprays to brighten up lightly shaded areas. Plant it at the rear of a large perennial border or use it in large sweeps around shrubs or at the edge of a woodland. Goat's beard also grows well on the shady side of a house; a dark wall shows off the white flowers. Good companion plants include the wild ginger *Asarum europaeum*, lungworts (*Pulmonaria*), and bleeding hearts (*Dicentra*).

GROWING AND PROPAGATION Grow in light shade, or sun in cool climates, and moist, rich soil. Goat's beard seldom needs division, but you can divide it if you want more plants.

Plant Profile

HARDINESS
Hardy

SEASON OF BLOOM
Summer

LIGHT REQUIREMENTS

MOISTURE REQUIREMENTS

HEIGHT
1 to 2m

SPREAD
1 to 1.5m

Asarum
WILD GINGER

The appealing heart-shaped leaves of this woodsy groundcover look cool and lush at the feet of shrubs or the edge of a shady garden.

Use European wild ginger as a low evergreen groundcover in wild, shaded areas for four-season interest.

Canada wild ginger, also known as the Canadian snakeroot, (*A. canadense*) can reach 30cm tall and bears lightly hairy, grey-tinted, heart-shaped leaves up to 15cm long.

A. *shuttleworthii* has heart-shaped evergreen leaves with white mottling. The purplish brown flowers are hairy and open in early summer. 'Callaway' is a vigorous cultivar that spreads to form an attractive groundcover to 20cm tall.

GARDEN USES Wild gingers are wonderful for providing evergreen foliage or groundcover in shady sites. They make handsome additions to wildflower gardens and good companions for other shade-loving flowers such as blue phlox (*Phlox divaricata*) and Virginian cowslips (*Mertensia pulmonarioides*).

GROWING AND PROPAGATION Wild ginger needs shade and moist, rich, well-drained soil. Spread leafmould, composted bark or rotted compost as a mulch around plants every year to maintain a high level of organic matter in the soil. To increase your supply of plants, divide in early spring. Handle the brittle roots carefully so you don't break them. In ideal locations, wild ginger may self-sow and spread moderately.

APPEARANCE Wild gingers have handsome, mostly evergreen leaves that can spread in colonies to form impressive sweeps of greenery. The ground-level flowers are small, rounded, dull red-purple and hairy. They are often hidden by the leaves.

A sarabacca, the European wild ginger A. *europaeum*, has shiny, evergreen, kidney-shaped leaves that form low masses to 20cm tall.

Plant Profile

HARDINESS
Hardy

SEASON OF BLOOM
Spring

LIGHT REQUIREMENTS

MOISTURE REQUIREMENTS

HEIGHT
15 to 30cm

SPREAD
30cm or more

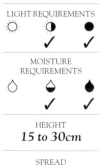

Asclepias tuberosa
BUTTERFLY WEED

Bring butterflies to your garden with the nectar-rich, incredible orange flowers of summer-blooming butterfly weed.

Butterfly weed has clusters of star-shaped orange flowers that open in early summer.

APPEARANCE Butterfly weed has flat-topped, rounded clusters of small orange flowers that butterflies adore. The flowers mature into slender upright pods with tapered ends. They open to release kid-pleasing seeds clad in downy parachutes. Butterfly weed grows from 30 to 90cm tall and has long, narrow leaves. Gay Butterflies Group is a mix of orange-, red-, and yellow-flowered plants that average 60cm tall.

GARDEN USES Use butterfly weed in the middle or back of a flower border where its upright shape contrasts nicely with low or mound-shaped plants. It is right at home in a sunny meadow garden too, Surefire companions include coreopsis and rudbeckias.

GROWING AND PROPAGATION Plant in full sun and average, well-drained soil. Remove the faded flowers in early summer to encourage rebloom in late summer but take care as the milky sap can cause skin irritation. Butterfly weed may self-sow; removing the seedpods will keep it in check. If you don't mind a few volunteer self-sown plants, leave the interesting seedpods in place instead of snipping them off. Butterfly weed grows from a carrotlike taproot that doesn't transplant well. For best results, start with young plants and leave them undisturbed in the garden. If you want to increase your supply of plants, take tip cuttings in late spring or early summer or sow fresh seed in a cold frame in the late autumn.

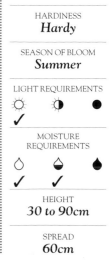

Plant Profile

HARDINESS
Hardy

SEASON OF BLOOM
Summer

LIGHT REQUIREMENTS

MOISTURE REQUIREMENTS

HEIGHT
30 to 90cm

SPREAD
60cm

Aster

ASTER, MICHAELMAS DAISY

These tough but beautiful daisylike flowers offer plenty of colour and height choices to add long-lasting, often late-season bloom to a sunny bed or border.

The glowing flowers of 'Alma Potschke' New England aster can warm the greyest autumn day.

There are several compact cultivars of Michaelmas daisies (*A. novi-belgii*), such as red 'Jenny' and white 'Kristina', that grow to 30cm tall.

GARDEN USES Use low autumn-flowering cultivars in the front of a flower border and tall cultivars at the back. They make ideal companions for artemisias and ornamental grasses. *A. × frikartii* is a great partner for *Rudbeckia fulgida* and *Sedum* 'Herbstfreude'. You can also include asters in a meadow garden.

GROWING AND PROPAGATION These asters all require full sun and average to fertile soil. Frikart's aster is best in well-drained soil with modest moisture. New England asters and Michaelmas daisies prefer evenly moist soil. Fertilize modestly or not at all. Use grow-through wire cages or rings to prevent tall asters from flopping. It also helps to pinch the new growth back a few centimetres in spring to encourage the plants to branch and stay compact.

New England and Michaelmas daisies may need to be divided every three years to renew growth and control their spread. *A. × frikartii* seldom needs division. Some asters are prone to powdery mildew, but some cultivars like 'Purple Dome' are usually mildew-free.

APPEARANCE Some species of asters have daisylike flowerheads. Others are full and rounded like a chrysanthemum.

Long-blooming Frikart's aster (*A. × frikartii*) has lavender daisylike flowers from summer into autumn on stems 30 to 90cm tall. 'Mönch' has blue flowers; 'Wonder of Staffa' has large blossoms.

New England asters (*A. novae-angliae*) have flowers of pink, white, lavender, and purple. They tend to be tall, averaging 1 to 1.5 metres. 'Andenken an Alma Pötschke', which has long-blooming pink flowers, grows 1 to 1.2 metres tall. One exception is the cultivar 'Purple Dome', which remains a compact 60cm tall and has rich, deep purple flowers.

Plant Profile

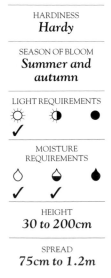

HARDINESS
Hardy

SEASON OF BLOOM
Summer and autumn

LIGHT REQUIREMENTS
☀ ◐ ●
✓

MOISTURE REQUIREMENTS
◇ ◈ ◆
✓ ✓

HEIGHT
30 to 200cm

SPREAD
75cm to 1.2m

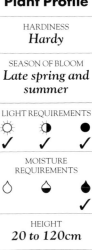

Astilbe
ASTILBE

Moisture-loving astilbes are a natural choice to plant beside a pond or water garden, where you can enjoy the reflections of their eye-catching flower clusters and rich foliage.

APPEARANCE Astilbes have erect or arching plumes of tiny flowers that brighten up any shady garden.

A. x *arendsii* hybrids grow from 60 to 120cm tall. Hybrids may bloom early, midseason, or late, and come in pink, white, cream, and red.

A. *simplicifolia*, with starry white flowers, reaches a petite 30cm tall. A. 'Sprite' has delightful light pink flowers.

Chinese astilbe (A. *chinensis* var. *pumila*) is a low, spreading plant with reddish foliage and deep pink flowers from 25 to 30cm tall late in summer. Another variety for late-summer bloom is A. *chinensis* var. *taquetii*, which can reach over 1 metre tall when in bloom. It is usually available as 'Purpurlanze' and has purple-tinged flowers.

A. *thunbergii* can reach 60 to 90cm tall and boasts handsome cascading pink flowers in mid- to late summer. 'Professor van der Weilen' is a white form.

GARDEN USES Use astilbes in a shady garden or on the shady side of a house or wall. Let them sweep around stream or pond banks. Use compact astilbes in the front of a flowerbed and taller ones toward the back. They look great with lungworts (*Pulmonaria*) and hostas. Astilbes also look lovely beneath trees or shrubs, but the soil needs to be damp because the tree

and shrub roots will compete for moisture.

GROWING AND PROPAGATION Plant in light shade and rich, moist soil (A. *chinensis* var. *taquetii* can tolerate occasional dry conditions). Astilbes will also grow well in sun but the soil must not be allowed to dry out. Brown leaf edges are a sign of underwatering. Mulch generously with compost and sidedress with well-rotted manure in spring. Divide as needed to control size and multiply your astilbe collection. If the clump becomes hollow in the centre, dig the centre out and discard, refill the space with rich soil, and allow the astilbe to fill in again.

'Fanal' is a compact, early-flowering hybrid of *Astilbe* x *arendsii* with deep crimson flowers.

Plant Profile

HARDINESS
Hardy

SEASON OF BLOOM
Late spring and summer

LIGHT REQUIREMENTS
☀ ◐ ●
✓ ✓ ✓

MOISTURE REQUIREMENTS
◇ ◒ ◆
✓

HEIGHT
20 to 120cm

SPREAD
60cm

Athyrium
LADY FERN, JAPANESE PAINTED FERN

Plant these gorgeous ferns along a path where their lacy fronds can be best admired.

Lady fern thrives in moist soils, forming dense mounds of delicate green fronds.

Plant Profile

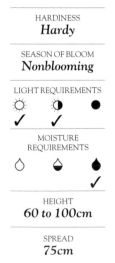

HARDINESS
Hardy

SEASON OF BLOOM
Nonblooming

LIGHT REQUIREMENTS
☀ ◑ ●
✓ ✓

MOISTURE REQUIREMENTS
◊ ◖ ◆
      ✓

HEIGHT
60 to 100cm

SPREAD
75cm

APPEARANCE These ferns have leafy fronds that are twice-divided, creating a full and delicate effect. In ideal conditions, they will spread to form large colonies.

Lady fern (*A. filix-femina*) has broad, soft green fronds growing gracefully upright to as tall as 1 metre.

Japanese painted fern (*A. niponicum* 'Pictum') has striking leaves tinged with purple and splashed with silver; new growth is a handsome lavender shade and the silver variegation glows in a shady woodland garden. Its arching fronds spread to 60cm and 75cm wide.

GARDEN USES Lady ferns are as lovely in a shady wall-side planting or in a woodland garden. Use them to offer interesting texture at the base of a tree trunk or include them among woodland flowers such as bloodroot (*Sanguinaria canadensis*), foamflowers (*Tiarella*), and blue phlox (*Phlox divaricata*).

GROWING AND PROPAGATION Plant in rich, moist soil in light shade; in permanently moist conditions, lady ferns can grow in sun. Mulch deeply with compost or leafmould to keep the soil constantly moist. Divide plants in early spring as new fronds are about to arise.

Baptisia australis
BLUE FALSE INDIGO

*Add height and interesting texture to perennial beds
with the cloverlike leaves and striking blue flowers of blue
false indigo.*

Blue false indigo flowers add valuable early-summer colour to a bed or border, but the blue green foliage is an asset too.

APPEARANCE Blue false indigo has spikes of bright blue flowers that rise from 60 to 120cm tall. The blue-green leaves, which resemble clover, were once fermented to produce a blue dye. The dark seedpods remain interesting long after the flowers have faded.

GARDEN USES Use blue false indigo in the middle or rear of a flower garden. The cool blue flowers are a perfect complement to pink peonies, bleeding hearts (*Dicentra*), and cranesbills (*Geranium*). They contrast nicely with silver artemisia foliage or with golden and orange flowers, such as fern-leaved *Achillea millefolium*.

GROWING AND PROPAGATION Plant in full sun and fertile, well-drained soil. In open or lightly shaded sites, let the plant grow up through a supporting ring or grid. Deadhead to encourage a long period of bloom or allow the seedpods to form for summer and autumn interest. This is one perennial that stays put in the garden and won't require division. To increase your supply of plants, take cuttings from the tips of stems after flowering ends.

Plant Profile

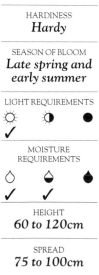

HARDINESS
Hardy

SEASON OF BLOOM
Late spring and early summer

LIGHT REQUIREMENTS
☀ ◐ ● ✓

MOISTURE REQUIREMENTS
◌ ◑ ● ✓ ✓

HEIGHT
60 to 120cm

SPREAD
75 to 100cm

Brunnera macrophylla
BRUNNERA

Enjoy the clear blue old-fashioned flowers of brunnera in early spring, then let the showy leaves fill in to command attention all season in a shady garden.

Brunnera has pretty blue spring flowers and grows well in moisty, shady spots.

Plant Profile

HARDINESS
Hardy

SEASON OF BLOOM
Mid to late spring

LIGHT REQUIREMENTS
☀ ◐ ●
   ✓

MOISTURE REQUIREMENTS
◌ ◖ ◆
  ✓ ✓

HEIGHT
30 to 45cm

SPREAD
60cm

GARDEN USES Use brunnera in large clumps or as an edging near the front of a shady flower or shrub border. It's an interesting companion to epimediums (*Epimedium*) and Japanese painted fern (*Athyrium niponicum* 'Pictum'). Brunnera also looks beautiful in a woodland garden with bloodroot (*Sanguinaria canadensis*), blue phlox (*Phlox divaricata*), and ferns.

GROWING AND PROPAGATION Plant in light shade and moist, rich but well-drained soil. In cool climates, brunnera can tolerate quite a bit of sun as long as the soil does not dry out. Help the foliage reach full size by keeping the soil moist and adding a generous layer of compost as a mulch. For more plants, divide in autumn or sow seed in early spring. Variegated brunneras are best left undisturbed.

APPEARANCE Cheerful sprays of blue flowers arise in mid to late spring along with many woodland flowers. When they fade, hairy heart-shaped leaves increase in size, reaching 30 to 45cm tall. They remain handsome for the rest of the growing season. Variegated cultivars with white-marked leaves, such as 'Dawson's White' or 'Hadspen Cream', are especially attractive and brighten up any shady spot.

Calamagrostis × *acutiflora*
FEATHER REED GRASS

*Add flair to a perennial garden on a moist site
with the vertical line and showy flowers of
feather reed grass.*

APPEARANCE Feather reed grass forms a dense, grassy clump that reaches about 60cm tall and may remain green year-round in mild climates. Feathery reddish flowerstalks grow to 1.5 metres tall, drying to a straw colour for winter. 'Karl Foerster' has upright foliage and pinkish brown flowers that remain colourful all summer.

C. × *acutiflora* 'Overdam' has white-variegated leaves and golden flowerheads to 1 metre tall.

GARDEN USES 'Karl Foerster' feather reed grass is nice in the middle or rear of a flower garden where it forms a billowing backdrop for perennial flowers. Combine it with pink summer bloomers, such as garden phlox (*Phlox paniculata*), Stokes' aster (*Stokesia laevis*), and pink balloon flower (*Platycodon grandiflorus*). You can also use this lovely grass as a low screen or in a gravel garden. Or plant it with tall perennials, such as rudbeckias and kniphofias, in a meadow-style border.

GROWING AND PROPAGATION Plant in moist but well-drained soil in full sun or light shade. Use a wide spacing to allow some elbowroom around the plant. If you want to cut back the flowerstalks and foliage, do so in early spring before new growth starts. Propagate by division in the spring or autumn.

The upright stems of 'Karl Foerster' feather reed grass add striking vertical accents to a perennial border.

Plant Profile

HARDINESS
Hardy

SEASON OF BLOOM
Summer

LIGHT REQUIREMENTS

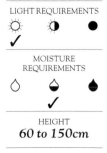

MOISTURE REQUIREMENTS

HEIGHT
60 to 150cm

SPREAD
60 to 100cm

Cimicifuga racemosa
BLACK SNAKEROOT

Liven up lightly shaded areas under trees with the white-flowered candles of this attention-getting maroon-stemmed flower.

Cimicifuga racemosa
'Atropurpurea', a relative of black snakeroot, has purplish leaves tapped by tall spikes of creamy white flowers.

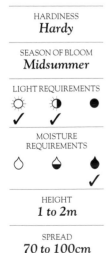

HARDINESS
Hardy

SEASON OF BLOOM
Midsummer

LIGHT REQUIREMENTS
☀ ◑ ●
✓ ✓

MOISTURE REQUIREMENTS
◇ ◐ ◆
✓

HEIGHT
1 to 2m

SPREAD
70 to 100cm

APPEARANCE Black snakeroot has long spires of small white flowers that tower 1 to 2 metres over the bushy, compound foliage. Bugbane (C. *japonica*), a related species, reaches 60 to 90cm tall and produces white flowers in late summer or early autumn.

C. *simplex* from Kamchatka flowers in autumn, reaching up to 1.5 metres high. 'White Pearl' is a compact version to 90cm tall.

GARDEN USES The tall white flower spikes provide an impressive upright accent for lightly shaded borders or woodland edges. Use black snakeroot for height around trees or in the rear of a mixed border. It makes a good partner for astilbes, hostas, and ferns.

GROWING AND PROPAGATION Plant in sun or light shade and moist, rich, well-drained soil. Remove faded flowerstalks after bloom is finished. The plants mature into a single large clump that will continue to grow well without being divided. If you want to increase your supply of plants, you can divide in the autumn; be sure that each division has at least one bud.

Convallaria majalis
LILY-OF-THE-VALLEY

*This old-fashioned charmer with fragrant flowers makes a
great groundcover for shady corners of the garden
where it's difficult to mow.*

Lily-of-the-valley bears charming bell-like flowers in spring. It spreads rapidly to form an attractive groundcover.

APPEARANCE Spikes of fragrant, white, bell-shaped flowers arise from paired, upright broadly sword-shaped leaves that spread into large colonies. Occasionally red berries may form. The plant, however, is poisonous so remove the berries before they attract the attention of young children. 'Albostriata' is a variegated lily-of-the-valley with leaves narrowly striped with cream.

GARDEN USES Lily-of-the-valley flowers are renowned for their fabulous perfume, which is wonderful in the garden. Let the plants spread across the front of shade gardens or serve as a groundcover beneath trees or shrubs. Lily-of-the-valley looks good with spring-flowering bulbs, such as tulips, and with early-flowering perennials, such as lungworts (*Pulmonaria*).

GROWING AND PROPAGATION Under ideal conditions of light shade and fertile, moist but well-drained soil, lily-of-the-valley will spread vigorously. It will also grow in full shade (especially in mild areas) and in sun in cool climates, and it will adapt to dry to average soils. If you interplant lily-of-the-valley with less aggressive plants, limit its spread with a root barrier, such as slates or a plastic edging strip. Divide in spring or autumn to keep in bounds and create new plants.

Plant Profile

HARDINESS
Hardy

SEASON OF BLOOM
Spring

LIGHT REQUIREMENTS
☼ ◑ ●
✓ ✓ ✓

MOISTURE REQUIREMENTS
◌ ◌ ◒
✓ ✓ ✓

HEIGHT
15 to 20m

SPREAD
30cm or more

Coreopsis
COREOPSIS, TICKSEED

Brighten a sunny garden with an armload of cheerful golden flowers from the versatile coreopsis clan.

'Grandiflora' is a cultivar of *Coreopsis verticillata*. It has an airy beauty, with soft mounds of foliage covered in starry yellow flowers.

APPEARANCE Coreopsis have bright yellow or golden flowers that bloom much of the summer.

C. *grandiflora* has elongated, often lobed leaves, reaches to 60cm tall, and bears great masses of big, deep yellow flowers. Cultivars include 'Early Sunrise' and 'Mayfield Giant'. The compact C. 'Goldfink' only reaches 24cm tall.

Lance-leaved C. *lanceolata* is similar to C. *grandiflora* and is sometimes confused with it. The popular hybrid C. 'Sunray' has double flowers.

C. *verticillata* has short, fine leaves and forms an airy mound up to 80cm tall. It has several cultivars including 'Moonbeam' with pastel yellow flowers and 'Zagreb', which has golden flowers and reaches only 45cm tall.

The pink tickseed C. *rosea* is a standout with pink flowers to 60cm tall and fine, needlelike leaves.

GARDEN USES Use coreopsis in any sunny situation that calls for a long-blooming perennial. They fit well into a foundation planting and are perfect for the front or middle of a flower border. They're also ideal in a meadow planting. All coreopsis combine well with *Salvia* × *superba* and blue balloon flower (*Platycodon grandiflorus*). In a garden of warm colours, plant coreopsis with crocosmias and butterfly weed (*Asclepias tuberosa*).

GROWING AND PROPAGATION Plant in full sun (C. *rosea* also grows in light shade), in average, well-drained soil. Stems may flop if the soil is too rich. Allow room around lance-leaved coreopsis plants to discourage powdery mildew. Divide coreopsis in spring or autumn if they are declining or to increase your supply of plants. Trim back faded flowers to encourage rebloom. Some coreopsis cultivars can flower until frost.

Plant Profile

HARDINESS
Hardy

SEASON OF BLOOM
Summer

LIGHT REQUIREMENTS
☀ ◑ ●
✓

MOISTURE REQUIREMENTS
◊ ◖ ◆
✓ ✓

HEIGHT
30 to 80cm

SPREAD
20 to 50cm

Corydalis lutea
YELLOW CORYDALIS

Try the fine-textured foliage of corydalis as a groundcover or filler in a shady garden and enjoy a bonus of yellow blooms.

Yellow corydalis blooms from spring until autumn, making it an invaluable addition for shady gardens with rich soil.

APPEARANCE Yellow corydalis has small, tubular, flowers and handsome blue-green compound leaves similar to columbines (*Aquilegia*). It can bloom for months. The flowers are lemon yellow and abundant on the spreading plant, which can reach to 40cm tall in bloom.

For a similar look with blue flowers, try C. *flexuosa* 'Blue Panda'. It reaches only 20cm tall and produces sky blue flowers through the growing season.

GARDEN USES Use yellow corydalis for a bright touch in the foreground of any shady garden, foundation planting, or woodland scene. It looks great with bleeding hearts (*Dicentra*), Brunnera (*Brunnera macrophylla*), ferns, and hostas.

GROWING AND PROPAGATION Plant in rich, moist but well-drained soil in light or full shade. Yellow corydalis can self-sow heavily. Allow the extra seedlings to expand the planting, or transplant them to a new site. Remove faded flowers occasionally to encourage rebloom and limit self-seeding.

Plant Profile

HARDINESS
Hardy

SEASON OF BLOOM
Late spring, summer, and autumn

LIGHT REQUIREMENTS
☼　◑　●
　　✓　✓

MOISTURE REQUIREMENTS
◌　◔　◑
　　✓　✓

HEIGHT
20 to 40m

SPREAD
45cm

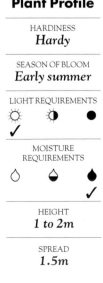

Crambe cordifolia
CRAMBE

Add flair to a sunny perennial border with the enormous leaves of crambe and its surprisingly delicate cloud of white flowers.

Crambe cordifolia has airy heads of white flowers that erupt in summer and then disappear when the spent flower stems are cut back.

Plant Profile

HARDINESS
Hardy

SEASON OF BLOOM
Early summer

LIGHT REQUIREMENTS
☼ ◐ ●
✓

MOISTURE REQUIREMENTS
◌ ◒ ◓
✓

HEIGHT
1 to 2m

SPREAD
1.5m

APPEARANCE *Crambe cordifolia* sports broad, toothed leaves to 60cm wide that spread into a large rosette up to 1.5 metres across. Airy sprays of small white flowers, like baby's-breath (*Gypsophila paniculata*), rise above the foliage, reaching 1 to 2 metres tall.

GARDEN USES Plant crambe in the rear or middle of a flower border for a magnificent flower display. The airy blossoms make a nice backdrop for upright flowers such as early meadow phlox (*Phlox maculata*) and *Salvia × superba*. Crambe retains its interesting bold leaves throughout the growing season.

GROWING AND PROPAGATION Plant in sun and rich, moist soil, allowing enough space for the plants to expand. Mulch in spring to retain the soil moisture. Stake the bloom stalks to keep upright and cut them back after the flowers fade. To make more plants you can divide crambe in spring or sow seed.

Crocosmia
MONTBRETIA

Make a firework display in your border with the vivid orange, red, and yellow spikes of crocosmia.

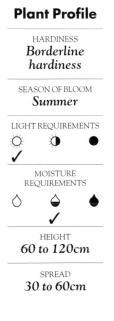

Fiery red 'Lucifer' crocosmia makes an eye-catching addition to beds and borders.

APPEARANCE Crocosmias have upright fans of foliage similar to Siberian iris (*Iris sibirica*) and bold spikes of gold, red, and orange flowers.

C. × *crocosmiiflora* grows up to 90cm tall. Its arching stems carry small flowers in orange or yellow, among grass-like leaves.

Some of the most magnificent crocosmias are hybrids such as C. 'Lucifer', which grows 1 to 1.2 metres tall and has vivid red flowers. Lemon 'Citronella' and pale orange-yellow 'Solfatare' are shorter as they grow up to 75cm tall.

GARDEN USES Use crocosmias for an upright accent among mounding and spreading perennials such as 'Moonbeam' coreopsis (*Coreopsis verticillata* 'Moonbeam'), daylilies (*Hemerocallis*), and Stokes' aster (*Stokesia laevis*).

GROWING AND PROPAGATION
Crocosmias grow from corms, similar to crocuses. Plant in spring, providing full sun and moist, rich well-drained soil. The corms will multiply, producing tight, showy clumps of plants. In cold areas apply a deep mulch over winter. Divide in the spring to renew the plants or to increase your supply. If red spider mites become a problem, spray them with insecticidal soap.

Plant Profile

HARDINESS
Borderline hardiness

SEASON OF BLOOM
Summer

LIGHT REQUIREMENTS

MOISTURE REQUIREMENTS

HEIGHT
60 to 120cm

SPREAD
30 to 60cm

Crocus
CROCUS

This group of bulbs includes both early spring bloomers and autumn-flowering types to accent perennial borders or to naturalize in the lawn.

Dutch crocuses planted in random clusters in your lawn will make a cheerful spring display.

Plant Profile

HARDINESS	*Hardy*

SEASON OF BLOOM
Early spring or autumn

LIGHT REQUIREMENTS
☼ ◐ ●
✓ ✓

MOISTURE REQUIREMENTS
◊ ◖ ◆
✓ ✓

HEIGHT
5 to 8cm

SPREAD
5 to 10cm

APPEARANCE Petite bowl-shaped flowers open on sunny early spring days. The foliage is narrow and straplike with a white stripe down the centre of each leaf. The earliest-blooming species have smaller flowers. They include C. *chrysanthus*, with cream to golden-yellow flowers, which grow to 5cm tall, and its cultivars, such as yellow 'Goldilocks', blue 'Blue Bird', and purple 'Skyline'.

Dutch crocus (C. *vernus*) and Dutch hybrid crocuses flower slightly later and often have larger blooms. They include cultivars such as lavender 'Enchantress', violet 'Vanguard', and 'Queen of the Blues'. The large, bright yellow C. 'Dutch Yellow' is 8cm tall. More unusual autumn-flowering species include the saffron crocus (C. *sativus*) and the showy C. *speciosus* with violet flowers appearing before the leaves.

GARDEN USES Plant crocuses at the perimeter of your lawn, beneath shade trees, or around spring-flowering shrubs. Put crocuses near a path, doorway, or window where you can enjoy their flowers first thing in spring. If you plant crocuses at a distance from your house, use brightly coloured, large-flowered types in big groups. Plant them in large sweeps between clumps of perennials such as daylilies and hosta. Use them in combination with larger bulbs such as daffodils by planting the crocuses in a shallow layer over the more deeply planted, larger bulbs.

GROWING AND PROPAGATION Plant crocuses in sun or light shade in average, well-drained soil. Crocuses grow from bulblike corms, which you plant in autumn. Let the crocus foliage die back before removing it; delay mowing if the crocuses are planted in the lawn. Divide if overcrowded or to expand your collection.

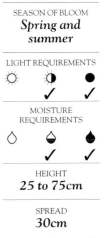

Dicentra
BLEEDING HEART

Remember yesteryear with the pretty foliage and dainty,
arching stems of pink or white bleeding hearts in your
favourite shady spot.

APPEARANCE Heart- or tear-shaped flowers are trademarks of this perennial. They emerge on arching stems over handsome compound foliage. One of the best is wild bleeding heart. (*D. formosa*), which reaches from 25 to 45cm tall. It produces modest but abundant pink tear-shaped flowers much of the spring and summer. 'Alba' has white flowers. The hybrid cultivar *D.* 'Luxuriant' grows 30 to 45cm tall and has red-pink flowers that are at their best in cool weather. Taller and more magnificent are *D. spectabilis* and its white form *alba*. These grow to 75cm or more.

Dutchman's breeches (*D. cucullaria*) can reach 30cm tall. It is peppered with small dangling white or yellowish white pouchlike flowers. It goes dormant in early summer and should be kept dry.

GARDEN USES Use bleeding hearts in the front or middle of any shade garden. They are naturals for wildflower gardens, where some species provide extended colour after spring bloomers fade. Combine bleeding hearts with wild gingers (*Asarum*), yellow corydalis (*Corydalis lutea*), *Epimedium ×* *versicolor* 'Sulphureum', and ferns.

GROWING AND PROPAGATION Plant in light to full shade in a protected position; in warm climates, morning sun is fine.

The delicate flower sprays and soft foliage of dicentra mix in beautifully with fern fronds.

Plant in moist, rich soil and mulch with compost. In dry summers the foliage may die down as the plant goes dormant. To increase your supply of plants, divide clumps in autumn or take root cuttings of *D. spectabilis*, also in the autumn.

Plant Profile

HARDINESS
Hardy

SEASON OF BLOOM
Spring and summer

LIGHT REQUIREMENTS

MOISTURE REQUIREMENTS

HEIGHT
25 to 75cm

SPREAD
30cm

Echinacea purpurea
ECHINACEA

Fill your summer gardens with this pink-purple daisy and you'll get a bonus of nectar-seeking butterflies and seed-eating goldfinches.

The pink petals of *Echinacea purpurea* 'Leuchtstern' seem to almost glow next to its rich orange-brown cones.

Plant Profile

HARDINESS
Hardy

SEASON OF BLOOM
Summer

LIGHT REQUIREMENTS

MOISTURE REQUIREMENTS

HEIGHT
60 to 120cm

SPREAD
30 to 60cm

APPEARANCE This American prairie plant has flashy red-purple petals surrounding an orange-red central cone. The flowering stems can reach 1.2 metres tall but seldom need staking for support. The pointed oval leaves are large and somewhat hairy. Once the flowers fade, the cones remain, becoming darker with maturity and attracting foraging birds when the seeds ripen. 'White Lustre' has white flowers. 'Leuchtstern' has rose-pink flowers. 'Magnus' has a dark central disk.

GARDEN USES Use echinaceas in the middle to rear of any sunny flower border. For a lovely trio, plant them with *Rudbeckia fulgida* and coreopsis or with balloon flowers (*Platycodon grandiflorus*) and Michaelmas daisies. You can also use echinaceas in combination with ornamental grasses and other prairie plants, such as sidalceas.

GROWING AND PROPAGATION Plant in full sun and average, well-drained soil. Irrigate during dry weather. Remove faded flowers to prolong bloom. The "cones" will add winter interest if you let them stand, and you'll get a bonus of self-sown seedlings in spring and summer. If you need more plants, simply transplant the seedlings. Plants often decline after division.

Epimedium
BARRENWORT, BISHOP'S MITRE

Try epimediums for a lovely groundcover that produces a flurry of small columbine-like flowers in a shade garden.

APPEARANCE The main attraction of epimediums is their handsome heart-shaped foliage, which often is tinted with red. The small flowers, shaped like a bishop's mitre or a jester's cap, are often hidden among the leaves; some gardeners clip the leaves short so the flowers will be easier to see.

Long-spurred E. *grandiflorum* reaches 20 to 35cm tall with pink, purple, or white flowers. Red epimedium (E. × *rubrum*) grows to 30cm tall with bronze-painted spring foliage that turns red and orange in autumn before dying down. It has red flowers with yellow spurs.

E. × *youngianum* reaches 20cm tall. Among its cultivars are 'Roseum', with pink flowers, and extra-early-flowering 'Niveum', with white flowers.

E. × *versicolor* 'Sulphureum' has soft yellow flowers on plants to 30cm tall or more.

GARDEN USES Epimedium's pretty, deciduous to evergreen foliage makes an attractive groundcover or edging for any shade garden. It grows especially well around trees and shrubs, where it's often difficult to establish groundcovers. Combine epimedium with spring-flowering bulbs such as daffodils and squills (*Scilla*) for a riot of spring colour and appealing greenery through the rest of the season.

GROWING AND PROPAGATION Plant in light to full shade and moist, fertile soil. Many epimediums can grow in less than ideal soil, even in dry sites riddled with woody plant roots. They spread slowly to colonize wide areas. To speed up their spread, divide plants in autumn and transplant. Cut back any tattered foliage in spring before growth resumes.

'Sulphureum' is a cultivar of *Epimedium* × *versicolor*. It has bronze-tinged leaves that look beautiful in the garden and also in cut flower arrangements.

Plant Profile

HARDINESS
Hardy

SEASON OF BLOOM
Spring

LIGHT REQUIREMENTS

MOISTURE REQUIREMENTS

HEIGHT
15 to 35cm

SPREAD
20 to 35cm

Eranthis hyemalis
WINTER ACONITE

Tuck winter aconite tubers under trees or at the front of perennial borders where it's easy to spot their low yellow flowers in early spring.

Winter aconites are such early bloomers that winter snow may linger beneath their yellow blossoms.

Plant Profile

HARDINESS
Hardy

SEASON OF BLOOM
Late winter, early spring

LIGHT REQUIREMENTS
☼ ◑ ●
✓

MOISTURE REQUIREMENTS
◊ ◖ ◆
✓

HEIGHT
10 to 15cm

SPREAD
10cm

APPEARANCE This petite, late winter bloomer has clusters of yellow buttercup-like flowers on stems 10 to 15 cm tall surrounded by a frill of divided foliage. The Cilicica Group are an old-fashioned aconite with bronze-tinged foliage, 10cm tall.

GARDEN USES Put large sweeps of winter aconites in the front of flower or shrub beds or swirl them around clumps of perennials such as Lenten rose (*Helleborus orientalis*), hosta, or Siberian iris (*Iris sibirica*). They look great with other early spring bulbs such as daffodils or purple and blue crocuses.

GROWING AND PROPAGATION Buy fresh tubers and soak briefly before planting. Plant winter aconite tubers in autumn, in light shade or sun, in rich, moist but well-drained soil. Winter aconites may flower poorly the first year after planting, but each year their display will improve. Once growing well, winter aconites may reseed and expand generously. After three or four years of growth, winter aconites are ready for dividing. To rejuvenate old clumps or increase your supply, divide clumps in spring before the leaves die down.

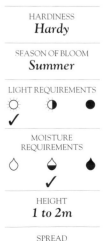

Eupatorium fistulosum
JOE-PYE WEED

The shrublike proportions and huge mauve flower puffs of Joe-Pye weed make a magnificent backdrop to a sunny perennial border.

Joe-Pye weed sports umbrella-like flower clusters in late summer.

APPEARANCE Lofty heads of red-purple flowers top stems of long leaves, which may appear in pairs along the purplish stems or encircle the stems in groups. Plants can grow up to 2 metres tall.

Joe-Pye weed (*E. purpureum*) ranges from 1 to 2 metres tall with clusters of pink or purple flowers up to 25cm across. *E. purpureum* subsp. *maculatum* has slightly smaller flowerheads and spotted or blotched stems. 'Atropurpureum' has huge purple-red flowerheads up to 30cm across.

GARDEN USES Use Joe-Pye weed in the rear of a flower border or in moist areas, where it makes an ideal companion to Siberian iris (*Iris sibirica*) and daylilies.

GROWING AND PROPAGATION Plant in full sun or light shade and rich moist soil. Joe-Pye weed seldom needs fertilizing. To reduce height, pinch back new growth in spring to encourage branching. Divide in autumn as needed to control spread or to increase your supply of plants. Deadhead to prevent self-sowing.

Plant Profile

HARDINESS
Hardy

SEASON OF BLOOM
Summer

LIGHT REQUIREMENTS
✓

MOISTURE REQUIREMENTS
✓

HEIGHT
1 to 2m

SPREAD
Clumps spread a metre or more

Geranium
CRANESBILL, HARDY GERANIUM

Plant a variety of cranesbills for weeks of cheerful blooms and intriguing foliage that offers great red or orange autumn colour.

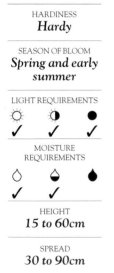

'Wargrave Pink' is a cultivar of *Geranium* × *oxonianum*. It makes a long-blooming groundcover that's perfect along a sunny pathway.

Plant Profile

HARDINESS
Hardy

SEASON OF BLOOM
Spring and early summer

LIGHT REQUIREMENTS
☼ ◐ ●
✓ ✓ ✓

MOISTURE REQUIREMENTS
◌ ◓ ◑
✓ ✓

HEIGHT
15 to 60cm

SPREAD
30 to 90cm

APPEARANCE Cranesbills are low-growing perennials that have saucer-shaped flowers and rounded leaves that may be lobed or finely cut. The common name cranesbill comes from the seedpod, which resembles the beak of a crane.

Vigorous G. × *oxonianum* has starlike leaves and bears pink flowers. It can reach 45cm tall. It has many cultivars including 'A.T. Johnson' with light salmon-pink flowers; 'Wargrave Pink' bears rich pink flowers.

Bloody cranesbill (G. *sanguineum*) grows to 30cm tall with bold purple-pink flowers and deeply cut leaves which colour well in autumn. Cultivars include 15-cm-tall 'Shepherd's Warning' with brilliant deep pink flowers and white 'Album'.

G. *renardii* has soft grey leaves and purple-veined white flowers to 20cm tall.

G. *maculatum* has light purplish pink flowers with a white centre and rises to 60cm tall.

Evergreen G. *macrorrhizum* forms a spreading groundcover with pink flowers to 40cm tall.

G. × *cantabrigiense* 'Biokovo' has pastel pink flowers and is usually evergreen. G. 'Johnson's Blue' has beautiful blue flowers on plants to 20cm tall.

GARDEN USES Use cranesbills in the front or middle of flower borders, around shrubs or small ornamental trees, or beside a path or retaining wall. G. *maculatum* looks great in a wildflower garden.

GROWING AND PROPAGATION
Cranesbills grow in sun to partial shade in almost any well-drained soil. Grey-leaf types need fast-draining soils. Clip faded flowers on 'Johnson's Blue' and G. × *oxonianum* cultivars to extend the flowering season. Divide in spring or late summer to control the spread of quick growers such as G. *macrorrhizum* or to increase your collection.

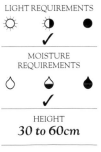

Helleborus
HELLEBORE

Get the jump on the garden season with hellebores,
which have beautiful foliage and roselike flowers that bloom
in winter and spring.

APPEARANCE The cheerful and showy bowl-shaped flowers appear very early in the growing season. The deeply lobed leaves are dark green and may be evergreen.

Corsican hellebore (H. *argutifolius*) is evergreen and can grow over 60cm tall with large clusters of spring green flowers.

Christmas rose (H. *niger*) reaches 30cm tall. In late winter to early spring it produces clear white flowers that fade to pink.

Lenten rose (H. *orientalis*) grows 30 to 45cm tall with white, green, pink, or purple flowers or combinations of these colours. The Lenten rose is very variable and there are huge numbers of cultivars and seedlings to choose from.

GARDEN USES Plant hellebores close to your house, patio, or path so you'll get maximum early-season enjoyment from the flowers. They also add a nice touch between shrubs in a mixed planting. Use the plants singly or in sweeps. Combine them with other early bloomers such as early-season daffodils, crocuses, squills (*Scilla*), and winter aconites (*Eranthis*).

GROWING AND PROPAGATION Plant in rich, moist but well-drained soil in light or medium shade. Cultivate the soil deeply before planting because hellebores produce a long taproot. Mulch in spring and autumn

to keep the soil moist, discourage weeds, and prevent the flowers from being stained by mud if they bow down near the soil. Corsican hellebore may need staking to hold the flowers upright. Remove tattered evergreen leaves at the end of winter. Avoid dividing or transplanting hellebores. If you need to increase your supply of plants, you can transplant any self-sown seedlings that may appear.

Lenten rose flowers in shades ranging from white to purple. If you want specific colours, buy plants in bloom.

Plant Profile

HARDINESS
Hardy

SEASON OF BLOOM
Winter and spring

LIGHT REQUIREMENTS
☼   ◐   ●
    ✓

MOISTURE REQUIREMENTS
◌   ◓   ●
    ✓

HEIGHT
30 to 60cm

SPREAD
30 to 45cm

Hemerocallis
DAYLILY

*Cover a slope with the lively green leaves and trumpetlike
flowers of daylilies, or use them as an accent in
borders and island beds.*

**Fast-
spreading
daylily** *H. fulva*
'Green Kwanso'
is a good choice
for a tough site
where touchier
perennials won't
grow well.

Plant Profile

HARDINESS
Hardy

SEASON OF BLOOM
*Late spring and
summer*

LIGHT REQUIREMENTS
☀ ◐ ●
✓ ✓

MOISTURE
REQUIREMENTS
◌ ◑ ●
✓

HEIGHT
35 to 150cm

SPREAD
60 to 100cm

APPEARANCE Open trumpet-shaped
flowers appear in spring and summer over
clumps of arching, straplike leaves. Plants
can grow from 30 to 150cm tall. You can
grow old-fashioned species such as tawny
orange-flowered *H. fulva* 'Green Kwanso'
or modern hybrids, which come in an
incredible variety of colours, shapes,
and sizes.

One of the earliest daylilies to flower
is *H. lilioasphodelus*. It has perfumed yellow
lily-like flowers on stems up to 1 metre tall.

Hybrid daylilies flower in shades of
yellow, orange, pink, red, green, ivory, and
purple. 'Pink Damask' is buff-pink; 'Helle
Berliner' is an off-white; 'Stafford' is
bright red. 'Stella de Oro' is a compact
60-cm-tall daylily with yellow-orange

flowers that flower throughout the
summer. 'Happy Returns', another
rebloomer, has lemon yellow flowers over
a long period. Miniature hybrids such as
'Mini Pearl' grow only 35cm tall.

GARDEN USES Use daylilies in any flower
or mixed border. Combine them with
Echinacea purpurea, butterfly weed
(*Asclepias tuberosa*), and gayfeathers
(*Liatris*) and grasses. Try planting spring-
flowering bulbs such as daffodils or tulips
around the perimeter of a daylily clump.
Use daylilies as groundcovers on banks or
other open areas.

GROWING AND PROPAGATION Daylilies
will thrive in a wide variety of soils and
exposures, from sand to clay and sun to
light shade. But an ideal site has sun and
moist, rich, well-drained soil. In light
shade, daylilies may flower less and be likely
to flop. Topdress with fertilizer in spring
and mulch with compost in autumn or
spring. In summer, remove faded flowers
and old flowerstalks to keep the plants tidy.
Divide fast-growing daylilies such as 'Stella
de Oro' every three years. Other types can
go for years without division. To divide a
mature clump, hose off the exposed roots
and saw apart the root mass with a sturdy,
sharp knife. Replant young, healthy
sections and compost the older parts.

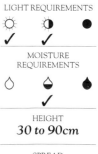

Heuchera
CORAL BELLS, HEUCHERA

Enjoy the delicate beauty of red and pink coral bells rising above neat scalloped leaves often richly coloured with a metallic sheen.

APPEARANCE Coral bells have dainty spikes of small bell-shaped flowers that bloom above a tidy rosette of usually evergreen leaves often beautifully marked.

Corals bells (*H. sanguinea*) produce white, pink, but usually red flowers that reach to 45cm tall over handsome scalloped leaves.

The Bressingham Hybrids come with white, pink, or red flowers, and *H.* 'Red Spangles' has green leaves and bright red flowers. All grow to about 45cm tall.

H. americana has leaves marked with brown and copper. It produces small green flowers on 50cm stems.

H. micrantha var. *diversifolia* 'Palace Purple' is one of the most beautiful of all foliage plants with purple or bronze leaves with a metallic sheen and white flowers.

GARDEN USES Use coral bells as an edging for any flower or shrub bed. Combine with other spring bloomers with attractive leaves, such as cranesbills (*Geranium*) and *Brunnera macrophylla*. Plant 'Palace Purple' with contrast colour perennials such as yellow coreopsis or silver-leaved artemisia.

GROWING AND PROPAGATION Plant in sun to partial shade and moist, rich, well-drained soil. Remove faded flower stems after blooming to keep the plants

neat and encourage a second flowering. The colour and quality of 'Palace Purple' can vary; look for vegetatively propagated forms with good purple foliage, and plant in light shade in warm climates to maintain the colour. Divide every 3 or 4 years, in autumn, to keep plants growing well.

Coral bells with bright pink flowers in late spring. They make a charming edging for perennial beds and borders.

Plant Profile

HARDINESS
Hardy

SEASON OF BLOOM
Summer

LIGHT REQUIREMENTS

MOISTURE REQUIREMENTS

HEIGHT
30 to 90cm

SPREAD
30 to 45cm

Hosta
HOSTA

*Depend on these unbeatable foliage
plants for cool elegance in your
shade gardens.*

Add excitement to shade gardens with variegated *Hosta fortunei* 'Albomarginata'.

APPEARANCE Hostas are renowned for their foliage – stylish leaves that range from small to gigantic, smooth-textured to puckered, in green, gold, blue, or white. There are hundreds of different types.

H. 'So Sweet' has white-edged leaves to 45cm tall with fragrant white flowers. 'Ginko Craig' has white-edged, lance-shaped leaves and purple flowers. 'Gold Standard' has yellow leaves which develop green margins with age.

H. *fortunei* grows to 60cm tall with long, heart-shaped leaves and soft lilac flowers. 'Albomarginata' has white-rimmed leaves.

H. *sieboldiana* var. *elegans* can reach 90cm tall with blue-green leaves and light lavender flowers in late summer.

H. *sieboldii* grows to 75cm tall with broad crinkled leaves.

H. *ventricosa* rises to 1 metre tall with large, heart-shaped leaves and blue-purple flowers.

GARDEN USES Use low-growing hostas as an edging or in clusters near the front of a flower or shrub garden. Larger hostas make bold accents rising above groundcovers such as the cranesbill *Geranium macrorrhizum*, epimediums, and foamflowers (*Tiarella*). Use large- to medium-sized hostas in the middle or back of a shady flower garden, with companions such as lady fern (*Athyrium filix-femina*) and wild bleeding heart (*Dicentra formosa*).

GROWING AND PROPAGATION Plant in light to full shade in moist, rich, well-drained soil. Once established, many hostas can withstand dry conditions. Fertilize in spring, and mulch with compost. If slugs are a problem, remove the mulch and trap slugs with beer traps (margarine tubs of beer set with the rim at soil level). Or surround your hostas with a layer of grit, which slugs will not cross. Hostas seldom need dividing, but you can multiply your collection by slicing off a rooted wedge from a mature plant in late summer.

Plant Profile

HARDINESS
Hardy

SEASON OF BLOOM
Summer

LIGHT REQUIREMENTS

MOISTURE REQUIREMENTS

HEIGHT
15 to 90cm

SPREAD
15 to 150cm

Iris sibirica
SIBERIAN IRIS

The commanding swordlike leaves and rich flower color of Siberian iris make a great accent in a perennial garden or a lush natural planting near a water garden.

APPEARANCE Flowers shaped like a fleur-de-lis are composed of three petals pointing down and three petals pointing up. They bloom abundantly over clumps of tall, grassy foliage. Plants can reach from 60 to 90cm tall. Siberian iris blooms in purple, lavender, blue, yellow, white, and red, plus combinations of these colours. 'Ruffled Velvet', a rich red-purple, reaches 50cm. 'Caesar's Brother' reaches 60cm with dark purple flowers. 'Butter and Sugar' is 70cm tall with white and yellow flowers. 'Shirley Pope' has deep purple flowers marked with white and grows to 80cm. 'Tycoon' with deep blue-purple flowers and 'White Swirl' grow to 90cm tall. Some new cultivars, such as red 'Reddy Maid', have thicker petals and stalks.

GARDEN USES Siberian irises are great in any flower garden, whether they're standing alone, in clumps, or in masses. Plant lower-growing types in the foreground and taller cultivars in the background. Their upright form contrasts well with mounded plants such as coreopsis and cranesbills (*Geranium*). They also grow beautifully on stream or pond banks combined with Joe-Pye weed (*Eupatorium*) and daylilies (*Hemerocallis*).

GROWING AND PROPAGATION Plant in full sun in moist, rich soil. They will also

tolerate light shade. Well-drained soil is best, but Siberian irises can tolerate occasionally wet soils. Slugs and snails can be a problem when new growth appears and aphids may attack the stem bases. Siberian irises need dividing every four years or so either after flowering or in early autumn; make sure each piece you replant has several shoots.

Siberian irises like 'Caesar's Brother' tolerate a wide range of conditions and thrive in almost any perennial border.

Plant Profile

HARDINESS
Hardy

SEASON OF BLOOM
Early summer

LIGHT REQUIREMENTS
☼ ◐ ●
✓

MOISTURE REQUIREMENTS
◌ ◑ ●
✓

HEIGHT
60 to 100cm

SPREAD
30 to 60cm

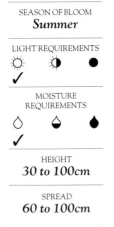

Lavandula angustifolia
LAVENDER

The wonderful fragrance of lavender's silvery foliage and blue-purple flowers is an extra treat in a sunny garden.

Lavender flowers attract butterflies and bees, and add beauty and fragrance to both cut and dried flower arrangements.

GARDEN USES Lavender is a natural choice for cottage or herb gardens where its fragrance is as important as its bright silvery grey foliage. Set it beside paths so it will release its perfume when you brush by. Plant a row of lavender plants together to form a low hedge. Combine with pink-flowered yarrow (*Achillea*), blue Russian sage (*Perovskia atriplicifolia*), and pink peonies, which provide contrast with their dark green foliage.

GROWING AND PROPAGATION Lavender needs full sun. It does best in fast-draining sandy soil. If you don't have sandy loam soil, plant lavender in a raised bed for good drainage, and amend the soil with coarse sand. You can also mulch with gravel to keep the base of the plant extra dry. In severe winter weather, cover plants with evergreen boughs or several layers of floating crop cover to limit damage. After new leaves emerge in spring, trim off any dead foliage. Prune to shape in autumn but do not cut into the old wood. Remove faded flower spikes to keep plants neat. Increase your supply of lavender by taking cuttings from the tips of new stems in late spring or summer and rooting them in pots.

Plant Profile

HARDINESS
Borderline to hardy

SEASON OF BLOOM
Summer

LIGHT REQUIREMENTS
☼   ◑   ●
✓

MOISTURE REQUIREMENTS
◊   ◖   ◆
✓

HEIGHT
30 to 100cm

SPREAD
60 to 100cm

APPEARANCE Bushy plants 60 to 100cm tall bear aromatic silver, needlelike leaves. Fragrant spikes of small flowers in blue, purple, or lavender arise in early to late summer; cultivars with white or pink flowers are less common, but available. Cultivars include 'Hidcote', which grows to 20cm tall and has purple flowers; 'Munstead', to 50cm with lavender flowers; and 'Jean Davis', to 45cm with light pink flowers.

Liatris
GAYFEATHER, BLAZING STAR

Vivid spires of intense purple-pink flowers make gayfeathers a natural choice for accenting a sunny bed or border.

APPEARANCE Gayfeathers have fluffy spikes of bright purple-pink flowers atop stems covered with grasslike leaves. White-flowered cultivars are available for most species.

L. *spicata* reaches 70 to 100cm tall with flower spikes about 60cm long in late summer and autumn. 'Kobold' (also known as 'Goblin') is a compact cultivar that grows to 50cm tall.

L. *scariosa* reaches over 1 metre tall with pale purple flowers in late summer and early autumn.

Kansas gayfeather (L. *pycnostachya*) grows 1 to 1.5 metres tall and blooms in summer into autumn.

GARDEN USES The upright form of gayfeathers stands out in the middle or rear of any flower garden. They contrast well with mounded or low-growing plants such as daylilies (*Hemerocallis*), cranesbills (*Geranium*), and *Scabiosa caucasica*. Try gayfeathers in combination with rudbeckias and Michaelmas daisies; the blooms also attract butterflies.

GROWING AND PROPAGATION Grow gayfeathers in sun and average, well-drained soil. In moist and fertile soils, stake the plants to prevent them from flopping over when in bloom. Slugs and snails may be a problem when the new

growth starts in spring. Gayfeathers seldom need division but if you need to expand your planting, you can divide in spring.

'Kobold' produces glowing mauve-pink blooms for several weeks beginning in late summer.

Plant Profile

HARDINESS
Hardy

SEASON OF BLOOM
Summer and autumn

LIGHT REQUIREMENTS
☀ ◑ ●
✓

MOISTURE REQUIREMENTS
◌ ◖ ●
  ✓

HEIGHT
50 to 150cm

SPREAD
30 to 60cm

Mentha
MINT

Mints have a delightfully refreshing scent, but they spread wildly, so plant them in a spot where they can extend their creeping stems at will, or contain them.

Mint has attractive flowers for cutting as well as aromatic foliage to spice up concoctions from your kitchen.

Plant Profile

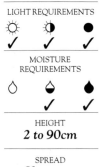

HARDINESS
Hardy

SEASON OF BLOOM
Summer

LIGHT REQUIREMENTS

MOISTURE
REQUIREMENTS

HEIGHT
2 to 90cm

SPREAD
Clumps to a metre

APPEARANCE There are dozens of aromatic mints; all have opposite leaves and square stems. They bear spikes of tiny, two-lipped flowers.

Variegated pineapple mint (M. *suaveolens* 'Variegata') smells more like apple and has handsome variegated leaves that reaches to 75cm tall.

Peppermint (M. ×*piperita*), 60 to 90cm tall, has smooth flavourful leaves and purple stems.

Spearmint (M. *spicata*) has toothed, lightly hairy leaves on stems that grow up to 90cm tall.

Corsican mint (M. *requienii*) is a ground-hugging type only 2cm tall.

GARDEN USES Use mints in shady herb gardens or as a quick-spreading groundcover for a moist, shady location. Try creeping Corsican mint between paving stones in a path or patio. Pineapple mint is less invasive than most mints and makes an appealing addition to the middle of a perennial border. It looks great with white Siberian irises (*Iris sibirica*) or meadow phlox *Phlox maculata* in a sunny garden, or with white-variegated hosta in a shade garden.

GROWING AND PROPAGATION Mints grow best in rich, moist soil and light to medium shade, but many will also thrive in full sun and less than ideal conditions. They are notorious spreaders that reroot from any broken pieces of stem or root left in the soil. To prevent rampant growth in a perennial garden, plant mints in bottomless buckets. Leave the pot rim 2 or 3cm above the soil surface, and check often to make sure the spreading stems don't escape (cut back any that do). Divide confined plants every two years to keep them vigorous.

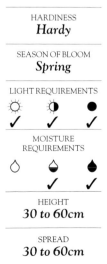

Mertensia pulmonarioides
VIRGINIAN COWSLIP

*Add the finishing touch to a shady border
with the gorgeous blue blossoms of this
unusual perennial.*

Virginian cowslips have dainty pink flower buds that change to blue as they open in spring.

APPEARANCE Clusters of nodding pink flower buds that open to blue bell-shaped flowers form at the top of the stems. The leaves are soft and oval. Plants reach to 60cm when in flower, then quickly die back to the ground until next year.

GARDEN USES Grow Virginian cowslips with other woodland flowers, such as bloodroot (*Sanguinaria canadensis*) and Solomon's seal (*Polygonatum*), on shady banks, near streams, and in moist places. Plant them between perennials such as ferns, cranesbills (*Geranium*), or hostas. When planted in a favourable site, Virginian cowslips can spread into a thick spring carpet of exceptional beauty.

GROWING AND PROPAGATION
Virginian cowslips thrive in light shade but can also grow in sun if the soil is moist. Provide fertile soil rich in organic matter and good drainage. Be sure to mark the location of the plants so you won't damage them by digging into them when they are dormant. The plants will self-sow as long as the soil isn't mulched heavily. To increase your supply of plants, divide large clumps after they flower.

Plant Profile

HARDINESS
Hardy

SEASON OF BLOOM
Spring

LIGHT REQUIREMENTS
☼ ◑ ●
✓ ✓ ✓

MOISTURE REQUIREMENTS
◌ ◍ ●
✓ ✓

HEIGHT
30 to 60cm

SPREAD
30 to 60cm

Miscanthus sinensis
MISCANTHUS

Plant long-lived Japanese silver grass to add structure and a sense of motion to a mixed border or pondside garden.

'Morning Light' is an excellent cultivar of *Miscanthus sinensis* that creates a fountain of white-edged foliage.

Plant Profile

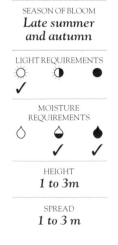

HARDINESS
Hardy

SEASON OF BLOOM
Late summer and autumn

LIGHT REQUIREMENTS

MOISTURE REQUIREMENTS

HEIGHT
1 to 3m

SPREAD
1 to 3 m

APPEARANCE This ornamental grass has clumps of upright leaves rising 1 to 3 metres tall. Feathery pink or red flower plumes open in late summer and autumn and ripen to soft tan, remaining attractive all winter. There are many fine cultivars to choose from. *M. sinensis* var. *purpurascens*, to 1.2 metres tall, has foliage that turns red in autumn and pink flowers in late summer. Compact 'Yakushima Dwarf' has silvery leaves and red flowers reaching to 85cm tall. 'Adagio' has silver-grey leaves

and grows only 60cm tall. 'Morning Light' grows to 1.2 metres tall with fine-textured, white-edged leaves.

M. *sinensis* 'Strictus' has yellow-banded leaf blades and a bold, upright shape to about 1 metre.

Zebra grass (M. *sinensis* 'Zebrinus') has similar yellow-banded blades but grows in an open shape to 1.5 metres tall.

GARDEN USES Silvery miscanthus provides beautiful movement in a perennial garden when the breeze rustles its long leaves and flower plumes. Most dry well to a buff colour and remain attractive deep into winter. Use them in the back of a flower or shrub garden, or make them a backdrop for perennials such as Siberian iris (*Iris sibirica*), Russian sage (*Perovskia atriplicifolia*), and 'Autumn Joy' sedum. They make instant summer privacy screens and special accents beside a stream or pond.

GROWING AND PROPAGATION Plant in sun and average, well-drained soil. Cut back old foliage to about 10cm tall in spring before growth resumes. Fertilize lightly in spring. To keep foliage in a tight clump, divide in the spring.

Muscari
GRAPE HYACINTH

Scatter grape hyacinths through bulb plantings and wildflower gardens for early spring colour of a delightful deep blue.

Muscari armeniacum sends up leaves in the autumn, and then blooms in early spring, producing grape-like blue flowers.

APPEARANCE Spikes of small bell-shaped flowers, 15 to 20cm tall, arise early in spring and continue to flower for weeks. Most cultivars have deep blue flowers, but there also are white and pink forms.

M. *armeniacum* is the standard blue grape hyacinth. It has several cultivars including 'Cantab' with lighter blue flowers. M. *botryoides* has bright blue flowers with a white rim; the form *alba* has scented white flowers.

GARDEN USES Plant large sweeps of grape hyacinths around clumps of perennials and shrubs. They look especially pretty with other spring bloomers such as lungworts (*Pulmonaria*) and Brunnera (*Brunnera macrophylla*). To create a mixed bulb planting, interplant grape hyacinth bulbs in a shallow layer between larger bulbs such as daffodils or tulips.

GROWING AND PROPAGATION Plant grape hyacinth bulbs in the autumn, in sun to light shade in average, well-drained soil. Mark the location of the bulbs so you don't disturb them when they're lying dormant in summer and autumn. To expand your planting, divide bulbs in early summer after the tops die back. You can divide grape hyacinths every four years.

Plant Profile

HARDINESS
Hardy

SEASON OF BLOOM
Spring

LIGHT REQUIREMENTS
☼ ◑ ●
✓ ✓

MOISTURE REQUIREMENTS
◊ ◖ ◆
✓

HEIGHT
15 to 20cm

SPREAD
3cm

Narcissus
DAFFODIL

Plant gorgeous handfuls of daffodil bulbs in your perennial garden for a spring show of cheerful blossoms that return year after year.

Miniature daffodils like 'Jack Snipe' are a good choice for mixed borders because the foliage dies back quickly after their delicate flowers fade.

Plant Profile

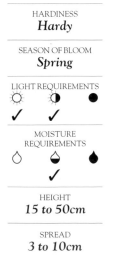

HARDINESS
Hardy

SEASON OF BLOOM
Spring

LIGHT REQUIREMENTS
☀ ◑ ●
✓ ✓

MOISTURE REQUIREMENTS
◌ ◓ ●
✓

HEIGHT
15 to 50cm

SPREAD
3 to 10cm

APPEARANCE Familiar trumpet flowers appear on upright stems in spring, in sunny yellow, white, orange, pink, or two-tones. Straplike leaves grow in upright clumps. While there are more than 50 naturally occurring species of daffodils, most of the popular cultivars are hybrids.

Traditional trumpet and large-cupped daffodils rise to 50cm tall. Some excellent cultivars include 'Salome', with a salmon trumpet ringed by white petals; all-white 'Mount Hood'; or 'Dutch Master', which has golden flowers.

Unusual hybrid double-flowered forms include fragrant white 'Cheerfulness' and 'Yellow Cheerfulness'. Species daffodils are smaller.

Triandrus daffodils such as white 'Thalia' and tazetta daffodils like pale yellow miniature 'Minnow' produce clusters of flowers on each flowering stem. Another popular miniature is golden 'Tête-à-Tête', which reaches 15cm tall.

GARDEN USES Use daffodils throughout flower and shrub gardens, planting sweeps of bulbs around clumps of daylilies (*Hemerocallis*) or hostas. They combine beautifully with blue-flowered Siberian bugloss (*Brunnera macrophylla*). Plant in large clumps of seven or more bulbs of a single cultivar for impressive colour. Plant trumpet daffodils in open woodlands or the edges of your lawn. For extended flowering season, plant early, midseason, and late cultivars.

GROWING AND PROPAGATION Plant bulbs in autumn in sun or light shade and average, well-drained soil. Topdress with compost after bloom to improve flowering on older plantings in borders. Allow the foliage to yellow before removing it. To renew a sparse-flowered planting, divide the bulbs as foliage dies back in summer. Mark location of bulbs to avoid damaging them while dormant.

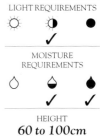

Osmunda regalis
ROYAL FERN

Add interesting colour accents and fine texture to moist, shaded gardens with the waist-high fronds of these beautiful ferns.

APPEARANCE Royal fern (*O. regalis*), which grows to over 1 metre tall, bears reddish-tinted young fronds that mature to green. Spore clusters form at the tips of the fronds. Several cultivars are available including 'Purpurascens' with fronds opening reddish-purple.

Cinnamon fern (*O. cinnamomea*) can grow from 60 to 100cm tall in a spreading vase shape. Showy stalks of cinnamon-coloured spore clusters come up first in the spring, followed by the yellow-green or dark green fronds.

Interrupted fern (*O. claytoniana*) is similar but stays about 60cm tall. The spore-bearing segments on each frond fall off early in the growing season, leaving a gap along the stalk.

GARDEN USES Use these ferns in moist woodlands, boggy locations, or by streams. They also are wonderful for shady mixed plantings beside perennials such as bleeding hearts (*Dicentra*) and corydalis.

Ferns like royal fern offer garden interest from the moment new fronds unfurl in early spring until they begin to die back in the autumn.

GROWING AND PROPAGATION Plant in light or partial shade and moist, rich, acidic soil. They will tolerate some sun and a neutral soil. Mulch with manure in spring, and keep cinnamon ferns and royal ferns uniformly moist. To increase your supply of plants, lift an established fern, and cut it into several sections in spring or autumn.

Plant Profile

HARDINESS
Hardy

SEASON OF BLOOM
None

LIGHT REQUIREMENTS
☀ ◑ ●
✓

MOISTURE REQUIREMENTS
◊ ◓ ●
✓ ✓

HEIGHT
60 to 100cm

SPREAD
60 to 100cm

Paeonia
PEONY

These old-fashioned favourites add lush, romantic blooms to a sunny garden in early summer, and their shrubby foliage makes a great backdrop for later-blooming perennials.

Peonies produce impressive shrublike mounds of sculptured foliage that are a garden asset even after the sumptuous blooms fade.

Plant Profile

HARDINESS
Hardy

SEASON OF BLOOM
Late spring and early to midsummer

LIGHT REQUIREMENTS
☀ ◑ ●
✓

MOISTURE REQUIREMENTS
◌ ◓ ●
✓

HEIGHT
45 to 75cm

SPREAD
45 to 90cm

APPEARANCE Peony flowers may be elegant singles, full doubles, or interesting intermediate forms. The large blooms top a vigorous clump of stems covered in handsome divided leaves. New leaves emerge as showy red shoots in spring. The flowers put on a great display for a week or two, and the foliage stays attractive all season, turning bronze in autumn.

Many popular peonies are hybrids of common peony (*P. officinalis*), which reaches 60cm tall and blooms in early summer, and *P. lactiflora*, up to 75cm tall and blooming slightly later. Both produce white, pink, or red flowers which often are fragrant.

Cultivars of the species have a wide range of flowering times, providing an extended peony season. Some classic cultivars of *P. lactiflora* include fragrant 'Sarah Bernhardt', a midsummer double pink, and 'Bowl of Beauty', a pink semidouble with an eye-catching centre of large golden stamens. 'Rubra Plena' is an early double red cultivar of common peony.

GARDEN USES Peonies are a great choice for the middle to rear of any flower border. Let them stand alone or in groups with cranesbills (*Geranium*), Siberian iris (*Iris sibirica*), and *Phlox maculata*. Draw attention to the red spring shoots by planting *Anemone blanda* or pasque flower (*Pulsatilla vulgaris*) around them.

GROWING AND PROPAGATION Plant in sun, in fertile, rich, moist but well-drained soil. Peonies can tolerate light shade, especially in warm protected positions. Fertilize with a balanced or high potassium organic fertilizer each spring. Support plants with a grow-through ring. During wet weather the flower buds may blacken and die from peony wilt caused by botrytis. To prevent spread, remove the diseased buds immediately and destroy the foliage in autumn. Peonies seldom need division and are best left undisturbed, but if you want more plants, you can lift clumps in late summer and divide by cutting them into sections using a sharp knife.

Perovskia atriplicifolia
RUSSIAN SAGE

*For an airy touch in a sunny perennial border, try the
silvery foliage and delicate blue flower spikes
of Russian sage.*

Russian sage
thrives on hot,
dry sites and its
silvery grey
stems remain
attractive long
after the flowers
fade.

APPEARANCE This bushy perennial grows
1 to 1.5 metres tall and produces long, slim
sprays of small blue flowers at the top of
the stems in late summer and early
autumn. The stems are covered with
small, toothed, silvery leaves that have a
mild sage fragrance. 'Blue Spire' has
abundant sprays of blue-purple flowers.

GARDEN USES Russian sage provides a
satisfying summer show when it blooms at
the rear of a large flower border. Set it
behind gold or pink yarrows (*Achillea*) and
pink or purple Michaelmas daisies (*Aster*).
You can also plant large masses of Russian
sage to create an informal hedge or screen
which has appeal in winter when the pale
stems stand out.

GROWING AND PROPAGATION Grow
Russian sage in sun and average, well-
drained soil. In harsh winters the stems
may get cut back by frost. If necessary, cut
the plant back to 30cm tall or less in spring
before growth resumes. In shadier sites,
stake the plant to keep it upright. Once
established, Russian sage tolerates heat
and drought. If you need more plants,
divide or take cuttings in spring.

Plant Profile

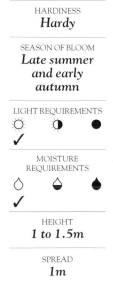

HARDINESS
Hardy

SEASON OF BLOOM
**Late summer
and early
autumn**

LIGHT REQUIREMENTS
✓

MOISTURE
REQUIREMENTS
✓

HEIGHT
1 to 1.5m

SPREAD
1m

Phlox
PHLOX

There's a phlox for every site in your garden – moss phlox to frost a slope with spring colour, garden phlox to anchor a border and wild blue phlox for shady gardens.

Blue phlox may die down in midsummer but will often regrow in the autumn.

reaches to 1.2 metres tall and flowers in white, pink, purple, salmon, and combinations of these colours. 'Fujiyama' has large heads of white flowers. Many cultivars are prone to powdery mildew.

GARDEN USES Use spring-flowering phlox as groundcovers or edgings for shrub or flower beds. Creeping phlox and blue phlox thrive in shade with other wildflowers such as Virginian cowslips (*Mertensia pulmonarioides*) and Solomon's seal (*Polygonatum*). Moss phlox is ideal for a rock garden, sunny bank, or groundcover. Summer-flowering phlox are perfect for the middle to rear of a flower border. Combine with low-growing cranesbills (*Geranium*) and autumn-flowering Michaelmas daisies (*Aster*) for a long-lasting colour sequence.

APPEARANCE All phlox species have tubular five-petaled flowers that flare out at the end to form a round face.

Spring-flowering phlox include creeping phlox (*P. stolonifera*), which grows to 25cm tall and has purple, lavender, white, or pink flowers; blue phlox (*P. divaricata*), which fans up to 35cm tall when its blue, white, or lavender flower sprays appear; and moss phlox (*P. subulata*), which forms dense mats to 10cm tall topped by pink, red, violet, or white flowers.

Meadow phlox (*P. maculata*) and perennial phlox (*P. paniculata*) bloom in summer. *P. maculata* has narrow foliage and clusters of pink or white flowers to 75cm tall. One great cultivar is pink-flowered 'Alpha'.

Garden phlox (*P. paniculata*)

GROWING AND PROPAGATION Grow wild blue phlox and creeping phlox in shade and moist, rich soil. Irrigate if needed during drought. Divide after flowering. Blue phlox may fall dormant in midsummer and regrow in autumn.

Grow moss phlox in full sun and average, well-drained soil. Plant early and garden phlox in moist, fertile, well-drained soil in full sun. Divide these summer-blooming phlox every four years to renew their growth.

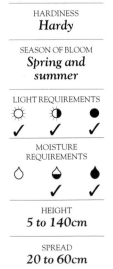

Plant Profile

HARDINESS
Hardy

SEASON OF BLOOM
Spring and summer

LIGHT REQUIREMENTS
☀ ◐ ●
✓ ✓ ✓

MOISTURE REQUIREMENTS
◌ ◔ ◕
  ✓ ✓

HEIGHT
5 to 140cm

SPREAD
20 to 60cm

Platycodon grandiflorus
BALLOON FLOWER

This enchanting perennial has beautiful blue-purple or pink star-shaped flowers that bloom all summer in a sunny garden, plus lovely yellow foliage in autumn.

APPEARANCE Balloon flower has remarkable inflated flower buds that look like miniature hot air balloons. They open to five-lobed, saucer-shaped flowers of rich blue or pink (the form *albus* has white flowers). The flowers cluster at the end of stems 30 to 60cm tall. The foliage is triangular and finely toothed. 'Fuji Blue' grows to 60cm tall. For a fuller flower, try 'Park's Double Blue', which reaches to 60cm tall. The compact variety *mariesii* stays 35cm tall. 'Fuji Pink' has pale pink flowers on 60-cm-tall stems.

GARDEN USES Balloon flowers are beautiful in the middle or rear of any flower garden. The unusual flower buds are a delight for both children and adults. Combine balloon flowers with garden phlox, Japanese anemones (*Anemone* × *hybrida*), and cranesbills (*Geranium*). They also look lovely against a backdrop of *Miscanthus sinensis* or with contrasting yellow yarrows (*Achillea*).

GROWING AND PROPAGATION Plant in full sun or very light shade and average, well-drained soil. Plants can become floppy if they receive too much shade and too much fertilizer. Mark the site of your balloon flowers in autumn, because they are late to emerge in spring and easy to damage by careless digging. Remove faded flowers to extend blooming season. Plants seldom need division, but if you want to make divisions to increase your supply of plants, you can lift clumps in spring or summer. If you do, dig deeply to avoid damaging the thick roots.

If you want a balloon flower for the front of a perennial border, choose the compact variety *mariesii*.

Plant Profile

HARDINESS
Hardy

SEASON OF BLOOM
Late summer

LIGHT REQUIREMENTS
☼ ◐ ●
✓

MOISTURE REQUIREMENTS
◌ ◔ ●
✓

HEIGHT
30 to 60cm

SPREAD
30 to 45cm

Polygonatum
SOLOMON'S SEAL

Add a grace note to a shady garden with the tall arching stems and dangling bell-like flowers of Solomon's seals.

White leaf outlines add an artistic touch to the gently curving stems of variegated Solomon's seal, *Polygonatum odoratum* 'Variegatum'.

APPEARANCE Solomon's seal has upright stems that arch at the top in a graceful curve. Attractive oval leaves cover the stems.

Great Solomon's seal (*P. biflorum*) can grow more than 2 metres tall and bears white, bell-shaped flowers that dangle from the underside of the arching stem.

The variegated Solomon's seal *P. odoratum* 'Variegatum' has eye-catching white-edged leaves, fragrant flowers, and stems to 60cm tall.

Common Solomon's seal (*P.* × *hybridum*) has much more upright stems. The cultivar 'Striatum' has cream striped leaves with an undulating, rather than smooth, surface.

GARDEN USES Let Solomon's seal provide an upright accent in your woodland shade or wildflower garden. The foliage lasts through the summer and the flowers mature into handsome dark blue berries, providing interest after other wildflowers and woodlanders have gone dormant. For a pleasant combination of shapes, plant colonies of Solomon's seal with creeping groundcovers like creeping phlox (*Phlox stolonifera*) and mound-formers like bloodroot (*Sanquinaria canadensis*).

GROWING AND PROPAGATION
Solomon's seal grows well in shade and moist, fertile soil that does not dry out in summer. Plants can expand to form thriving colonies. Divide in early spring to restrict their size or expand your planting.

Plant Profile

HARDINESS
Hardy

SEASON OF BLOOM
Spring and early summer

LIGHT REQUIREMENTS
☼ ◑ ●
  ✓ ✓

MOISTURE REQUIREMENTS
◌ ◓ ◉
  ✓ ✓

HEIGHT
30 to 200cm

SPREAD
60 to 120cm

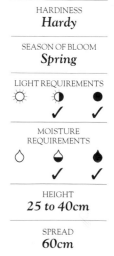

Pulmonaria
LUNGWORT,
JERUSALEM SAGE

Brighten the front of a shady garden with lungwort's striking silver-spotted foliage and soft blue spring flowers.

The narrow leaves of the long-leaved lungwort *Pulmonaria longifolia* offer an interesting backdrop for its vivid spring flowers.

APPEARANCE Lungworts produce small, bell-shaped blue or pink flowers in spring. They continue to please garden visitors through the rest of the growing season with long oval- or lance-shaped foliage, which can last into winter in mild climates. The foliage of some species also has attractive silver markings.

Jerusalem sage (*P. saccharata*), to 35cm tall, has pink buds and blue flowers. 'Mrs Moon' has exceptional silver-marked leaves.

Soldiers and sailors (*P. officinalis*) has pink and blue flowers. 'Sissinghurst White' is a white-flowered cultivar with lovely silver-spotted leaves.

The hybrid cultivar *P.* 'Roy Davidson' has long narrow leaves mottled with silver and grows to 25cm tall. The flowers open pink and turn to blue.

GARDEN USES Let lungworts carpet garden areas, spreading around the base of shrubs and trees or stretching across the front of borders. They work well as a shady groundcover especially if you can enjoy the silver-marked foliage from your windows. Good companions include daffodils, tall astilbes, blue-leaved hostas, and Japanese painted fern (*Athyrium niponicum* 'Pictum').

GROWING AND PROPAGATION Plant in shade, in moist, rich soil. In dry weather plants may go dormant prematurely. Leaves may mildew or turn brown around the edges if water is scarce. Divide as needed in spring to renew growth or expand your planting.

Plant Profile

HARDINESS
Hardy

SEASON OF BLOOM
Spring

LIGHT REQUIREMENTS
☼ ◐ ●
✓ ✓

MOISTURE REQUIREMENTS
◌ ◔ ◆
✓ ✓

HEIGHT
25 to 40cm

SPREAD
60cm

Rudbeckia
CONEFLOWER,
RUDBECKIA

Coneflowers have vibrant yellow flowers that carry a wave of colour through the summer in a sunny garden.

Rudbeckias
offer a long display of striking yellow flowers when planted in a warm, sunny spot with average soil.

APPEARANCE Rudbeckias have showy golden petals surrounding a dark centre cone. Hairy oval- to lance-shaped leaves cover the upright stems.

R. *fulgida* can grow to 1 metre tall. They bloom for about four weeks in mid- to late summer. The variety *sullivantii* 'Goldsturm' produces larger flowers on stems 60cm tall. If you want uniform plants, avoid mixed selections of seeds, and buy only plants of a named cultivar.

R. *laciniata* grows to 1.2 metres tall with leaves up to 10cm long. 'Goldquelle' is shorter, with shaggy, pale yellow double flowers. 'Herbstonne' can reach 2 metres tall and blooms in mid- to late summer. The flowers have yellow petals and a green cone.

GARDEN USES Rudbeckias work well in the middle to rear of any sunny flowerbed and look wonderful with *Salvia × superba*. You can mix rudbeckias with butterfly weed (*Asclepias tuberosa*), *Echinacea purpurea*, and gayfeathers (*Liatris*) in a meadow-style border. Put groups of three or five rudbeckias between shrubs to brighten them up in autumn. The long-lasting seedheads attract birds and provide winter interest.

GROWING AND PROPAGATION Plant in full sun and average, well-drained soil. In rich soil, plants may become floppy and require staking. Remove faded flowers often to encourage extended bloom. But leave late-season flowers in place so their dark cones will add to your garden's winter display. Rudbeckias may self-sow; remove faded flowers if you can't find space for more seedlings. Plants spread moderately. Divide in spring or autumn to increase your plant supply or to control growth.

Plant Profile

HARDINESS	*Hardy*
SEASON OF BLOOM	*Summer and autumn*
LIGHT REQUIREMENTS	☼ ◑ ● ✓
MOISTURE REQUIREMENTS	◌ ◑ ● ✓
HEIGHT	*45 to 200cm*
SPREAD	*60 to 80cm*

Salvia
SALVIA, SAGE

Include salvias in sunny borders for bold
colour and handsome mounds
of aromatic foliage.

APPEARANCE Salvias are shrubby or mounded plants that have square stems, oval or lancelike leaves, and small tubular flowers that cluster at the stem tips.

S. × *superba* grows to 90cm tall with leathery, triangular leaves and upright spikes of blue-violet flowers in summer.

S. *nemorosa* 'East Friesland' (sold as 'Ostfriesland'), a compact favourite, grows to 45cm tall.

Common sage (S. *officinalis*) is an evergreen culinary herb with lance-shaped silver leaves and blue flowers. It can grow to 60cm tall. 'Berggarten' has round leaves, 'Purpurascens' has purplish leaves. 'Tricolor' blends pink, white, and green in its leaves. 'Icterina' has gold variegated foliage and is less hardy than the species.

You'll also find many lovely cultivars of S. × *sylvestris*. 'May Night' (also sold as 'Mainacht') has dark purple flowers to 40cm tall. 'Rose Queen' has pink flowers to 60cm or more tall.

GARDEN USES Garden sages are at home in any herb garden. You can also use them in flower gardens to add aroma and foliage colour. Try S. *officinalis* 'Purpurascens' with yellow daylilies (*Hemerocallis*) or coreopsis. S. × *superba* is a great choice for the middle of a flower border. It blends well with creeping plants such as bugle

(*Ajuga*) and cranesbills (*Geranium*) or mound-shaped plants such as 'Moonbeam' coreopsis and 'Autumn Joy' sedum.

GROWING AND PROPAGATION Plant sages in sun and well-drained soil. Garden sages do best in fast-drying, sandy soil of low fertility, especially during winter. S. × *superba* grow well in average soils. Remove faded flower spikes promptly on S. × *superba* and it will rebloom. Divide plants in spring or autumn to control spread. To increase your supply of plants, take basal cuttings in spring or early summer.

'May Night' a cultivar of *Salvia* × *sylvestris*, produces intense blue-purple flower spikes in summer. Deadhead fading flowers promptly to encourage continued bloom.

Plant Profile

HARDINESS	*Hardy*
SEASON OF BLOOM	*Summer*

LIGHT REQUIREMENTS
☼ ◐ ●
✓

MOISTURE REQUIREMENTS
◊ ◖ ◆
✓

HEIGHT
30 to 90cm

SPREAD
30 to 90cm

Sanguinaria canadensis
BLOODROOT

Scatter bloodroot in shady woodland gardens or formal shade borders for white starry flowers in early spring.

Bloodroot has pristine white flowers that appear for a few days in early spring and attractive foliage that lasts into autumn.

Plant Profile

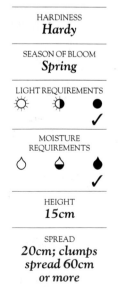

HARDINESS
Hardy

SEASON OF BLOOM
Spring

LIGHT REQUIREMENTS

MOISTURE REQUIREMENTS

HEIGHT
15cm

SPREAD
20cm; clumps spread 60cm or more

APPEARANCE In sunny spring weather, white, bowl-shaped flowers emerge from inside the fold of a large, lobed, blue-green leaf. When the weather turns dark, cold, or wet, the leaf encloses the flowers again. This dainty perennial grows to 15cm tall and can spread to form large colonies. The foliage can last into summer, providing interesting greenery in a shady garden. Double-flowered 'Plena' has long-lasting flowers that look like water lilies.

GARDEN USES Use clusters or sweeps of bloodroot in shady borders or around spring-flowering shrubs or trees. Ideal companions include Virginian cowslips (*Mertensia pulmonarioides*), cranesbill *Geranium maculatum*, and Solomon's seals (*Polygonatum*).

GROWING AND PROPAGATION Plant in a shady site with moist, rich, but well-drained soil. If you plant bloodroot under trees, avoid sites that are heavily riddled with roots, because the soil there can become dry and infertile. Irrigate during dry weather to prevent the foliage from dying back prematurely. Divide to increase your supply of plants in spring, after flowering is over.

Scabiosa caucasica
PINCUSHION FLOWER, SCABIOUS

Plant a cluster of these lacy-flowered perennials in a sunny garden and enjoy the pastel blossoms and the butterflies they attract.

Scabious look equally lovely in the garden and in cut flower arrangements.

APPEARANCE Flat, lacy flowerheads in blue, pink, or white appear from mid- to late summer over basal clusters of fuzzy, lance-shaped leaves. Plants can reach to 60cm tall; *alba* is a white-flowered variety.

S. 'Butterfly Blue' has greyish foliage and lavender-blue flowers to 30cm tall that appear most of the growing season. S. 'Pink Mist' is similar with purple-pink flowers.

GARDEN USES Use groups of three, five, or more scabious in the front or middle of a flower garden. Plant a large mixed cluster of 'Pink Mist' and 'Butterfly Blue' for an impressive display. Scabious also complement lavender or artemisias well. Or for contrast, try 'Butterfly Blue' with low-growing yellow daylilies (*Hemerocallis*).

GROWING AND PROPAGATION Grow scabious in sun and average, well-drained soil. Remove faded flowers to encourage extended bloom. Divide in spring only if needed to renew growth. To increase your supply of plants, take basal stem cuttings in spring.

Plant Profile

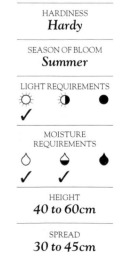

HARDINESS
Hardy

SEASON OF BLOOM
Summer

LIGHT REQUIREMENTS
☀ ◑ ●
✓

MOISTURE REQUIREMENTS
◊ ◊ ◆
✓ ✓

HEIGHT
40 to 60cm

SPREAD
30 to 45cm

Scilla
SQUILL

Tuck dozens of these early-blooming bulbs under shrubs and trees where their starlike blue, pink, or white flowers will lift your spirits in spring.

Siberian squills carpet the ground with intense blue blossoms in spring. Use them in beds, borders, and container plantings.

Plant Profile

HARDINESS
Hardy

SEASON OF BLOOM
Spring

LIGHT REQUIREMENTS
☼ ◐ ●
✓ ✓

MOISTURE REQUIREMENTS
◊ ◖ ◆
✓

HEIGHT
15cm

SPREAD
5cm

APPEARANCE Siberian squills (*S. siberica*) bear nodding, blue, star-shaped flowers on stems to 15cm tall. Each bulb also produces three or four strap-shaped leaves, which turn yellow and die by early summer. 'Spring Beauty' is a classic blue-flowered cultivar. 'Alba' has white flowers.

Spanish bluebells (once considered a species of Scilla, but now classified as *Hyacinthoides hispanica*) look similar to Siberian squill, but each bulb sends up a sprawling clump of basal leaves and several flowerstalks up to 45cm tall. The fragrant leaves may be blue, pink, white, or violet.

GARDEN USES Use squills to paint sweeps of spring colour across the front of garden beds. Combine them with other early spring bloomers such as winter aconites (*Eranthis hyemalis*), crocuses, and Lenten rose (*Helleborus orientalis*). Both squills and Spanish bluebells thrive in woodland gardens.

GROWING AND PROPAGATION Grow squills in sun to light shade and average, well-drained soil. In ideal conditions, squills will self-sow and spread in drifts. You can also enlarge a planting by dividing and replanting the bulbs every 4 years as the foliage dies back in summer.

Sedum
SEDUM, STONECROP

Creeping sedums trailing over a rock wall soften the wall's sharp edges, while tall sedums lend four-season interest in perennial beds and borders.

APPEARANCE All sedums have fleshy leaves and clusters of small, star-shaped flowers. Creeping types grow from 3 to 15cm tall, while upright sedums may reach 60cm tall.

Three excellent creeping sedums are *S. album*, *S. kamtschaticum*, and *S. spurium*. *S. album* bears evergreen leaves and white flowers.

S. kamtschaticum has yellow flowers and slim, scalloped leaves that may take on red tints in autumn. The cultivar 'Variegatum' has cream-edged leaves and flowers that turn orange with age.

S. spurium produces a carpet of round leaves, topped by pink flowers. Leaves of 'Variegatum' are coloured green, pink, and white. 'Dragon's Blood' (sold as 'Schorbuser Blut') has bronze foliage and red flowers.

The iceplant (*S. spectabile*) rises up to 45cm tall in an open vase shape. It has large heads of pink or red flowers. 'Stardust' has white flowers.

Sedum 'Autumn Joy', now sold as *S.* 'Herbstfreude', has fleshy round, toothed leaves and broccoli-like buds that open to pink flowers that turn bronze as they dry. Both remain attractive through the winter.

GARDEN USES Use low-growing sedums as groundcovers or edgings in sunny beds and gravel gardens. They also look nice creeping over stone retaining walls or

'Autumn Joy' sedium makes a great early autumn statement with its rounded, blue-tinged leaves and pink-blushed flowers.

spreading beside stone paths. Taller types are great in the middle of flower borders. Combine them with 'Stella de Oro' daylily (*Hemerocallis*), yuccas, ornamental grasses, and blue, purple, or white Michaelmas daisies (*Aster*). Try clumps of three or five in sunny open areas between shrubs.

GROWING AND PROPAGATION Plant in sun to light shade and average well-drained soil. Creeping types will also grow in light shade. Taller types need sun; if planted in fertile soil and shade they will flop. To encourage 'Autumn Joy' and 'Ruby Glow' to be self-supporting, pinch back growth in spring. Divide creeping sedums as needed in spring or autumn to control size. To increase your collection, divide plants or take cuttings of non-flowering stems in spring.

Plant Profile

HARDINESS
Hardy

SEASON OF BLOOM
Spring, summer, and autumn

LIGHT REQUIREMENTS
☀ ◑ ●
✓

MOISTURE REQUIREMENTS
◌ ◍ ◖
✓ ✓

HEIGHT
3 to 60cm

SPREAD
40 to 100cm

Stokesia laevis
STOKES' ASTER

*Plant drought-tolerant Stokes' asters in a
well-drained sunny bed for soft colour
that lasts for weeks.*

Stokes aster
is ideal for the
front of a sunny
border and
makes a great
cutting flower
too.

APPEARANCE Stokes' asters have
lavender, blue, or white flowers that look
like cornflowers with their fluffy centre.
Flowers rise to 60cm tall over a mound of
long, slender leaves. They are pleasantly
showy and bloom for months. 'Blue Star'
has pale blue flowers and reaches 40cm
tall. 'Alba' has white flowers to 60cm tall.

   A rosette of leaves may persist over
the winter months.

GARDEN USES Use Stokes' asters in the
front or middle of a flower border. Plant
clusters of at least three plants of a single
cultivar for the most attractive effect.

Blue Stokes' asters with *Rudbeckia fulgida*
and *Salvia × superba* make a great long-
blooming combination.

GROWING AND PROPAGATION Plant in
sun and average, well-drained soil.
Slugs and snails may hide in overwintering foliage. Remove faded
flowerheads from the plants periodically
to encourage extended period of bloom.
Plants seldom need division, but if you
want to increase your supply of Stokes'
asters, you can do so by lifting and
dividing plants in the spring.

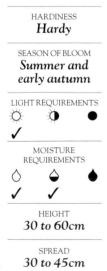

Plant Profile

HARDINESS
Hardy

SEASON OF BLOOM
**Summer and
early autumn**

LIGHT REQUIREMENTS
☼　◑　●
✓

MOISTURE
REQUIREMENTS
◊　◊　◊
✓　✓

HEIGHT
30 to 60cm

SPREAD
30 to 45cm

Tiarella
FOAMFLOWER

Blanket a shady corner with the attractive lobed leaves and misty flower clusters of this dainty groundcover.

Frothy foamflower, *Tiarella cordifolia,* offers white spring flowers and fast-spreading foliage that turns a pretty red in the autumn.

APPEARANCE Foamflower *T. cordifolia* has fuzzy spikes of small white or pastel pink flowers that arise over a rosette of maple-like leaves. The evergreen foliage remains attractive through the summer and turns reddish in autumn and winter. This foamflower can spread into a handsome groundcover to 25cm tall.

T. polyphylla has white flowers up to 20cm tall and forms a spreading clump.

T. wherryi looks similar to *T. cordifolia* but has pink or white flowers and forms a tidy clump that only gradually increases in size over the years. The foliage develops red markings in winter.

GARDEN USES Foamflowers look wonderful with other spring flowers in a woodland garden. Try them in sweeps with snowdrop anemone (*Anemone sylvestris*), Dutchman's breeches (*Dicentra cucullaria*), and bloodroot (*Sanguinaria canadensis*) for a mix of white flowers of different shapes. You can also let *Tiarella cordifolia* creep across the front of any shady bed or front garden. Foamflowers also look great with hostas and Japanese painted fern (*Athyrium niponicum* 'Pictum').

GROWING AND PROPAGATION Plant foamflowers in partial to full shade and moist, rich, but well-drained soil. Mulch them in spring with rotted manure or compost. Divide plants in spring or autumn to limit their spread or to increase your supply of plants. Or, you can remove rooted runners from *T. cordifolia* and *T. wherryi* and replant them anytime during the growing season providing you keep them watered.

Plant Profile

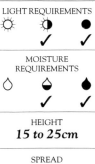

HARDINESS
Hardy

SEASON OF BLOOM
Late spring to early summer

LIGHT REQUIREMENTS

MOISTURE REQUIREMENTS

HEIGHT
15 to 25cm

SPREAD
60cm or more

Tulipa
TULIP

*Try some species tulips as well as familiar hybrid tulips
for colourful and varied spring displays.*

**One of the
dainty
species tulips**
you may want to
sample is *Tulipa
clusiana* var.
chrysantha.

Plant Profile

HARDINESS
Hardy

SEASON OF BLOOM
Spring

LIGHT REQUIREMENTS
☀ ◑ ●
✓

MOISTURE
REQUIREMENTS
◊ ◒ ◆
✓ ✓

HEIGHT
10 to 75cm

SPREAD
10cm

APPEARANCE Handsome six-petalled,
bowl-shaped flowers in yellow, red, pink,
white, orange, purple, and bicolours arise at
the top of slender stalks. Tulip species and
cultivars vary in shape, height, and
flowering time. Most types have broad,
pointed leaves. The following is only a small
sample of what's available for gardens.

T. tarda has narrow straplike leaves
and star-shaped white flowers with a
yellow centre. It reaches only 10cm tall.

Greigii tulips (*T. greigii*, varieties,
and hybrids) reach 25cm tall, bloom early
to midseason, and have purple-striped
foliage. 'Red Riding Hood' is red;
'Corsage' is rose and yellow; 'Sweet Lady'
is apricot and off-white.

Fosteriana tulips (*T. fosteriana*,
varieties, and hybrids) reach 30 to 40cm
tall and bloom early. They include
'Orange Emperor', 'Madame Lefeber', and
'Purissima'.

Kaufmanniana tulips (*T.
kaufmanniana*, varieties, and hybrids) grow
to 15 to 20cm tall and bloom very early.
They often have stripes on the outside of
the flower. 'Johann Strauss' is red and
yellow; 'Heart's Delight' has dark carmine
petals edged with pale pink and yellow at
the base.

GARDEN USES Use tulips in informal
groups between perennials such as
cranesbills (*Geranium*), peonies, and
daylilies (*Hemerocallis*). Plant seven, nine,
or more of a single cultivar per group to
give an impressive show. Choose early and
midseason cultivars for an extended
period of bloom. Try planting species
tulips with late-blooming daffodils and
early perennials.

GROWING AND PROPAGATION Plant
tulip bulbs in autumn in a sunny site and
fertile, well-drained soil. The ideal site is
dry in summer and moist in spring and
autumn. Species tulips can thrive for
years. Hybrid tulips bloom well only for a
year or two. After that, replant fresh bulbs.
Remove the foliage when it turns yellow.

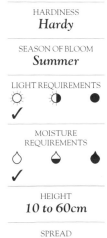

Verbena
VERBENA

Let verbenas weave their way around and between other sun-loving perennials to create a carpet of rich purple, pink, or white flowers.

'Homestead Purple' verbena has masses of dazzling purple flowers that last from early summer until frost.

APPEARANCE Small tubular, often fragrant, flowers that flare out into starry shapes appear in showy clusters through much of the growing season. The flowers arise at the end of stems covered in handsome, finely cut or lobed leaves.

V. corymbosa reaches up to 60cm tall, with tiny purple flowers which are sweetly fragrant. It spreads to form a groundcover.

Moss verbena (V. tenuisecta) grows to 25cm tall with prolific purple, mauve or white flower clusters. It also has a white-flowered form, *alba*.

There are several excellent hybrid cultivars among them. 'Homestead Purple', which bears purple flowers the entire growing season.

GARDEN USES Use creeping verbenas to edge sunny flower gardens or as a groundcover in sunny shrub beds. They also are great companions for taller perennials such as *Miscanthus sinensis*, 'Powis Castle' artemisia, and rudbeckias.

GROWING AND PROPAGATION Grow creeping verbenas in sun and average well-drained soil except for V. corymbosa which likes a moist soil. Cut back lanky stems occasionally to keep the plants compact and encourage rebloom. Mulch with straw or bracken to protect plants over winter. To increase your collection and provide replacements for winter losses, take stem cuttings anytime during the growing season.

Plant Profile

HARDINESS
Hardy

SEASON OF BLOOM
Summer

LIGHT REQUIREMENTS
☼ ◐ ●
✓

MOISTURE REQUIREMENTS
◇ ◗ ◆
✓

HEIGHT
10 to 60cm

SPREAD
30cm or more

Viola
VIOLET

These demure cottage garden favourites can spread to cover large areas in light to full shade, forming a groundcover that's attractive long after the spring flowers fade.

Sweet violet blooms in early spring. The heart-shaped leaves spread to form an attractive groundcover.

Plant Profile

HARDINESS
Hardy

SEASON OF BLOOM
Spring

LIGHT REQUIREMENTS
☼ ◑ ●
✓ ✓ ✓

MOISTURE REQUIREMENTS
◊ ◕ ◆
  ✓ ✓

HEIGHT
3 to 30cm

SPREAD
May spread to 30cm or more

The horned violet or viola (*V. cornuta*) reaches 15cm tall with white or lilac flowers.

The yellow wood violet (*V. biflora*) stays low, to 8cm tall and tolerates shade.

Dog violet (*V. riviniana*) grows to 20cm tall, and has purple flowers. The Purpurea Group have highly ornamental purplish leaves.

Sweet violet (*V. odorata*) is a cottage garden favourite with fragrant flowers. 'Alba' has white flowers with a yellow centre. *V.* 'Royal Robe' has purple blossoms.

GARDEN USES Use violets to edge a moist sunny, lightly shaded or woodland border. They look charming near lady fern (*Athyrium filix-femina*) and *Phlox divaricata*. The foliage remains handsome long after the flowers are gone. You can also let violets form a groundcover around shrubs or the base of tall perennials such as *Cimicifuga racemosa*, Solomon's seals (*Polygonatum*), and ferns.

APPEARANCE Violet flowers have two upright petals and three spreading lower petals. Flowers may be white, blue, purple, or yellow, depending on the species. All have handsome heart-shaped leaves. Some grow in low clusters; others rise on weak stems.

GROWING AND PROPAGATION Plant in moist, rich, well-drained soil in sun or light to full shade. Violets spread by creeping stems and by seed. You may need to transplant or weed out seedlings if they appear too prolifically. Divide in the spring or autumn to control spread or increase your collection of violets.

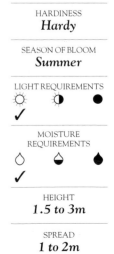

Yucca filamentosa
ADAM'S-NEEDLE, YUCCA

The bold daggerlike leaves and tall white flower spires of sturdy yucca plants accent softer perennials in a sunny garden.

Yucca has evergreen foliage that can withstand hot and dry conditions.

APPEARANCE Tall spikes of white, bell-shaped flowers appear over rosettes of upright, sharp-tipped, swordlike leaves. The evergreen leaves are blue tinted and reach to 75cm tall. The flower spikes may stretch to 1.5 metres or taller. 'Bright Edge' has gold-edged leaves and shorter flower spikes. 'Variegata' has blue-green leaves with cream margins, tinged with pink.

GARDEN USES Use Adam's-needles for their bold form, interesting evergreen foliage, and durability in hot, dry sites. Mix them into flower and shrub borders, or plant on a sunny patio. They look good singly or in clusters of three. Try planting them with a surrounding carpet of *Phlox subulata* and with bold companions such as ornamental grasses and rudbeckias.

GROWING AND PROPAGATION Plant in sun to light shade and lean to average, well-drained soil. Remove faded flower stems to keep the plants tidy. In time yuccas produce lateral shoots at the base of the plants. It's easy to remove these offshoots in spring and replant to increase your collection.

Plant Profile

HARDINESS
Hardy

SEASON OF BLOOM
Summer

LIGHT REQUIREMENTS
☼ ☼ ●
✓

MOISTURE REQUIREMENTS
◇ ◐ ◆
✓

HEIGHT
1.5 to 3m

SPREAD
1 to 2m

INDEX

Page numbers in *italics* refer
to illustrations and photographs

Y

Z

CREDITS

Susan McClure is an author, lecturer and garden designer from Valparaiso, Indiana.
She has written several gardening books, including *Successful Organic Gardening: Perennials*.

Bobbie Schwartz is a landscape consultant and designer and the owner of Bobbie's Green Thumb in Shaker Heights, Ohio.
She also gives lectures on landscape use of perennials and ornamental grasses.

Robin Siktberg is a garden designer and horticulturist with a special interest in perennials.
She is also a freelance writer, lecturer and photographer and lives in Chesterland, Ohio.

Alexander Apanius is a horticulturist and landscape designer and the owner
of Alexander A. Apanius, Inc., of Hudson, Ohio. He is the former director of the Cleveland Botanical Garden.

Photographic Credits

Key: *a* = above   *b* = below   c = centre   *l* = left   *r* = right

Defenders Ltd 90; Alan and Linda Detrick © 1996 ALD photo inc 44*r*, 94, 105, 118, 119, 123, 129, 144; Garden Matters 72*c*;
Hozelock plc 82; Jerry Pavia 8, 21, 33*b*, 37, 44*l*, 48, 49*a*, 54*b*, 56, 59, 66, 68 *l c*, 95, 97, 98, 100, 101, 102, 104, 106, 108, 109,
113, 114, 117, 122, 125, 126, 127, 128, 130, 132, 133, 135, 137, 138, 139, 140, 141, 146, 147, 148, 150, 151, 153; Joanne Pavia
99, 152; Photo/Nats Inc. 149 (Liz Ball), 60, 120 (Gay Bumgarner), 116 (Robert E. Lyons), 134 (Ann Reilly); Positive Images 7
(Margaret Hensel), 15 (Pam Spaulding), 33*a* (Harry Haralambou), 45, 80, 91*a* (Patricia J. Bruno), 49*b*, 70*b*, 89, 111 (Jerry
Howard), 54*a*, 70*a* (Les Campbell), 74*b* (Lee Lockwood), 78, 110 (Karen Bussolini), 91 *ac* (Jacob Mosser); Rodale Stock Images
69*r*, 76, 77, 91*bc*; Bobbie Schwartz 96; Robin A. Siktberg 74*a*, 103, 107, 112, 115, 131, 142; Harry Smith Horticultural
Photographic Collection 31, 72*a* & *b*, 83, 121, 124, 136, 145; Peter Stiles 13, 42, 143; Juliette Wade 2; Bob Woods 57.

All other photographs are the copyright of Quarto Publishing plc.